Big Al

John Gardiner

A Samuel French Acting Edition

SAMUELFRENCH-LONDON.CO.UK
SAMUELFRENCH.COM

Copyright © 1977 by John Gardiner
All Rights Reserved

BIG AL is fully protected under the copyright laws of the British Commonwealth, including Canada, the United States of America, and all other countries of the Copyright Union. All rights, including professional and amateur stage productions, recitation, lecturing, public reading, motion picture, radio broadcasting, television and the rights of translation into foreign languages are strictly reserved.

ISBN 978-0-573-08048-7

www.samuelfrench-london.co.uk

www.samuelfrench.com

FOR AMATEUR PRODUCTION ENQUIRIES

UNITED KINGDOM AND WORLD
EXCLUDING NORTH AMERICA
plays@SamuelFrench-London.co.uk
020 7255 4302/01

Each title is subject to availability from Samuel French,
depending upon country of performance.

CAUTION: Professional and amateur producers are hereby warned that BIG AL is subject to a licensing fee. Publication of this play does not imply availability for performance. Both amateurs and professionals considering a production are strongly advised to apply to the appropriate agent before starting rehearsals, advertising, or booking a theatre. A licensing fee must be paid whether the title is presented for charity or gain and whether or not admission is charged.

The professional rights in this play are controlled by Samuel French Ltd, 24-32 Stephenson Way, London NW1 2HD.

No one shall make any changes in this title for the purpose of production. No part of this book may be reproduced, stored in a retrieval system, or transmitted in any form, by any means, now known or yet to be invented, including mechanical, electronic, photocopying, recording, videotaping, or otherwise, without the prior written permission of the publisher. No one shall upload this title, or part of this title, to any social media websites.

The right of John Gardiner to be identified as author of this work has been asserted by him in accordance with Section 77 of the Copyright, Designs and Patents Act 1988

THE ORIGINAL CAST

THE BUMS

RICHARD WHITMORE
Al Capone

ROBIN LILLEY
Politician, Film Director, Ryan O'Hara, Boxer Hymie Weiss, Ticker-Tape Kid, Tony Lombardo, Coochee Cruiser, Alcatraz Jailbird Lucas 9752

ROGER HAWKINS
Politician, Florida.J.Candy, Speakeasy Guy, John Gusik (Capone's legal and financial wizard)

EAMONN QUINN
Frankie Caponi, The Coogan kid, Boxer, Cake Killer, Genna's brudder, Ticker Tape kid, Coochee Cruiser, Gino Shoe-Shine, Alcatraz Jailbird 69500

MICHAEL EVERITT
Bank Manager, Smilin' Boy O'Hara, Big Diamond Jim Colosimo, Angelo Genna, Ticker Tape Kid, Rudy the Masseur, Alcatraz Jailbird Vernon 98827

BILL WEEDON
Natty Frank Yale, Lefty Louie, Dion O'Banion, Ticker Tape Kid, Warder Johnston

PETER RUSSELL
Keystone Cop, Boxer, Officer O'Flaherty, Jacob Geiss, Ticker Tape Kid, Coochee Cruiser, Italian Tenor, Defence Counsel Aherné, Dr Twitchell.

BRIAN HULL
Restaurant Owner, Johnny Torrio, Sam Samoots Amatuna, Ticker Tape Kid, Judge Wilkerson, Alcatraz Jailbird Lindley 888

GRAHAM HOUGHTON
Gabriel Caponi, Torrio Torpedoe, Gino Gyp the Blood, Alberto Anselmi (Capone Torpedoe) Alcatraz Jailbird Perooski 57833

KIRK FOSTER
O'Hara Gangster Goofball, Boxer, John Scalise (Capone Torpedoe) Alcatraz Jailbird Rapp 88860

THE BROADS

MAUREEN PAYNE
Mae Coughlin (Capone's wife)

KATIE GOLDIE
Oobee Doobee Goil, Goldie Kandinski

EDITH PRATT
Liberty, Torrio Torpedoe, Bootleg Baby, Genna's brudder, Ticker Tape Kid, Coochee Cruiser, Courtroom Citizen

ANNIE WILKINSON
Oobee Doobee Goil, Bootleg Baby, Bugs Moran, Ticker Tape Kid, Coochee Cruiser, Eliot Ness

VAL COLES
Janitor, Gangster O'Hara, Boxer, Lily Lush, Klondyke O'Donnell, Ticker Tape Kid, Coochee Cruiser, District Attorney Johnson.

HEATHER GORDINE
Oobee Doobee Goil, Bootleg Baby, Miles O'Donnell, Ticker Tape Kid, Coochee Cruiser, Sob Sister One.

SALLY HULL
Teresa Caponi, Bootleg Baby, Genna's brudder, Sob Sister Two.

BARBARA GARDINER
Scraps the dog, O'Hara Gangster Squirt, Boxer, Bootleg Baby, Genna's brudder, Joe Howard, Ticker Tape Kid, Coochee Cruiser, G-Man.

JENNY RUSHBROOK
Politician, Cultural Creepess, Bootleg Baby, Genna's brudder, Ticker Tape Kid, Coochee Cruiser, Sob Sister Four.

WENDY WHITMORE
Oobee Doobee Goil, Bootleg Baby, Polack Joe Saltis, Ticker Tape Kid, Ed Konvalinka, Coochee Cruiser, Sob Sister Three.

FIRST HALF

EXHIBITS

ONE	The Spiel
TWO	In the Beginning
THREE	The Immigrant
FOUR	Al's First Job
FIVE	Cupid's Bow
SIX	Torrio's Night School
SEVEN	Outside the Pink Pineapple Speakeasy
EIGHT	Big Jim's Boithday Party
NINE	The Raid
TEN	On the Road

SONGS

'Kind Kinda Guy' AL & THE COMPANY
'Gonna Bend a New Shape' TERESA, GABRIEL, FRANKIE & THE COMPANY
'Muckraker's March' AL & THE COMPANY
'Stoney Broke Blues' NATTY FRANK YALE & THE OOBEE DOOBEE GOILS
'A Little Knuckle Knowledge' AL, JOHNNY TORRIO, GOLDIE & THE COMPANY
'Bootleg Baby Train' THE BOOTLEG BABIES' MAE & GOLDIE
'Big Jim's Chorale' THE COFFIN CHORISTERS
'Drivin Along on Love' MAE, AL & COMPANY

SECOND HALF

ELEVEN	The Share Out
TWELVE	Numero One
THIRTEEN	The Taking of Cicero
FOURTEEN	Death of O'Banion
FIFTEEN	Miami
SIXTEEN	Happy Valentine's Day
SEVENTEEN	The Untouchables
EIGHTEEN	The Trial
NINETEEN	Alcatraz
TWENTY	The Big Sleep

'Chicago City' AL, MAE, SCALISE, ANSELMI & GUSIK & THE COMPANY
'That Ole Slick Ticker-Tape Rag' THE TICKER TAPE KIDS
'Sailin' on the Sooper Salty Sea' THE COOCHEE CRUISERS
'Never 'til Now' MAE
'Rhadames Aria' from 'Aida' THE ITALIAN TENOR
'Alcatraz Blues' AL & THE JAILBIRDS
'Chicago City' (Reprise) THE COMPANY

A MAP OF THE CITY OF CHICAGO SHOWING GANG TERRITORIES

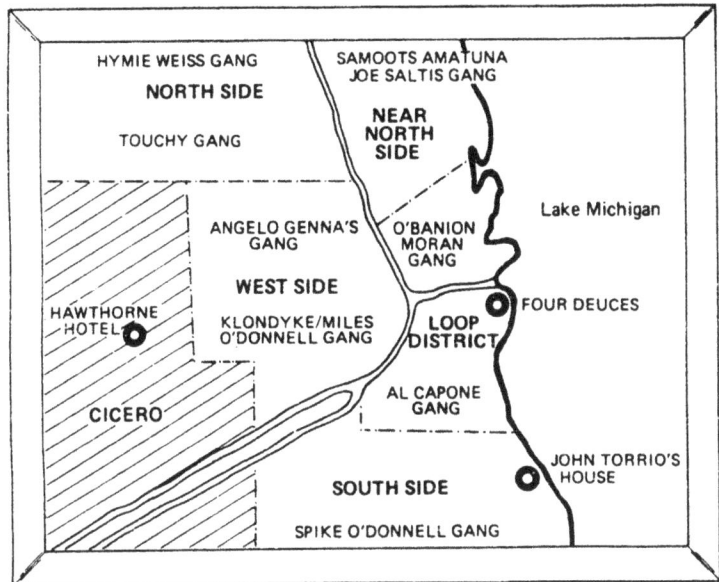

QUOTES

'I was T..T. until Prohibition' – *Groucho Marx*.
'O'Banion's head got away from his hat' – *Al Capone*.
'Perhaps after all, America never has been discovered. I, myself, would say that it had merely been detected' – *Oscar Wilde*.
'We must keep Chicago and America whole, safe and unspoiled' – *Al Capone*
'Cicero is virgin territory for whorehouses' – *Capone to Chicago Tribune*.
'The kids in Chicago are playing a new game – cops and cops' – *Chicago Tribune*.
'Chicago is unique. It is the only completely corrupt city in America' – *Alderman Merriman*.
'Prohibition booze was nothing short of wood alcohol squirted from a syringe into green beer and was called with affectionate revulsion-coffin varnish, craw, rot, rot gut, panther piss, busthead, razors, tarantula juice, strike me dead and sheep dip' – *Allsop*.

NOTES

The set consisted of an empty stage with scaffolding supplying five different playing areas. The scaffold area covered the upstage area. There were no ladder complications – the company climbed to areas at speed adding their own business to the scaling process.

Sub machine guns were hired from Bapty & Co. of London. They fired .38 blanks. These guns give a very realistic blaze and flare when fired. Full details concerning licence from Bapty's.

The lamps used in the Valentine Day Massacre were transported in **Supermarket shopping trolleys**. Such trolleys were also used to hold the Bootleg Baby Booze and incorporated in the Bootleg Baby Train Choreography.

Costumes are up to individual directors but a basic with simple additions are best especially in the opening twenty minutes of the First Half when there are so many changes of scene. **Props and Scenery** were all cartoon in style and either flown or carried. Very bright colours, light and one dimensional.

In the middle of the central playing area in the First Half was a shooting target with a dollar money sign in the centre, high stage left an advert for CIGARS and right from top to bottom of scaffold an advert for NEW YORK TIMES. In the second half these were reversed to reveal the target shattered by bullet holes with the words Rat-tat-tat across it – cigars became GOILS and NEW YORK TIMES became CHICAGO TRIBUNE.

Simple maroons (mini maroons) or rim shots can help with the exploding of the ticker tape group. A tower was not used a la script but just one side of the scaffold area. The KIDS were in white T shirts and jeans and entered like clockwork robots.

SET PLAN
NOT TO SCALE

CARS

CARS HAND HELD/HARDBOARD CUT OUTS

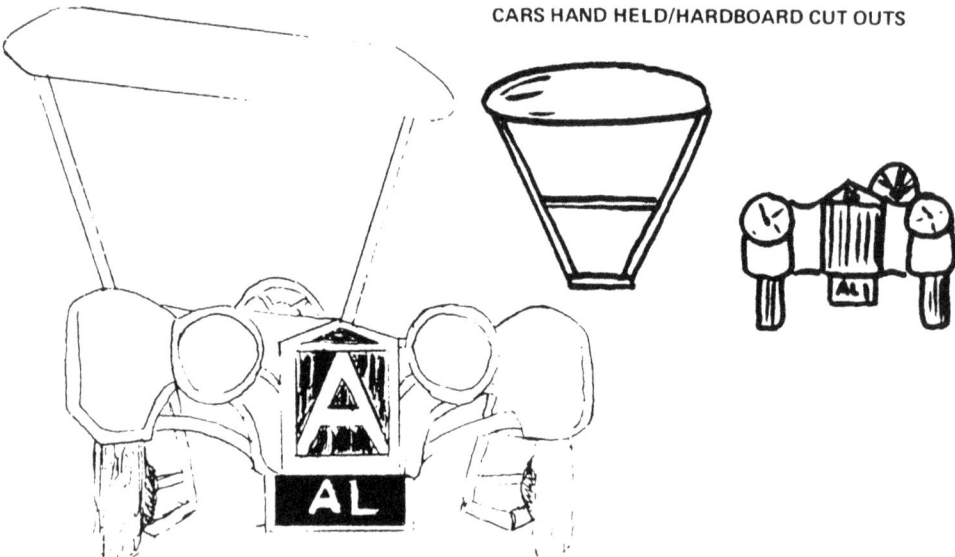

FIRST HALF

EXHIBIT ONE 'THE SPIEL'

As the HOUSE LIGHTS go down the stage is empty and dark — in the silence our attention is drawn to the NEWSPANEL on which the following message is flashed

> NEWSPANEL ... AL CAPONE ... PUBLIC ENEMY NUMBER ONE ...

After the message has flashed across we hear very loud machine gun fire followed by police sirens and screams etc. During this barrage of sound the company burst onto stage — they are dressed as a motley of city dwellers, gangsters, bums, hoboes, pimps etc. They are in a panic of fear, we hear phrases like 'Lets get the hell outa here'. They scatter to set places on the scaffold set and stage (See SET DESIGN). They create a variety of twenties period shapes and angles. A police whistle silences the noise and the company FREEZE. The LIGHTS that have been going on and off hold at pre-set for opening. The COMPANY are lit by pools of light. They sing one of the following words although the continuous total should resemble a sentence spoken by one voice

SUNG MUSIC CUE

1	THIS	10	ED
2	IS	11	EST
3	THE	12	AND
4	STOR-RY	13	RICH
5	OF	14	EST
6	AL	15	MAN
7	CAPONE	16	OF
8	THE	17	HIS
9	WICK	18	TIME

This is followed by a chord when the company change their group shape and position

SPOKEN

<u>ONE</u>: This is the story of Al Capone ... a story about ...
<u>TWO</u>: Cops!
<u>THREE</u>: Gangsters!
<u>FOUR</u>: Molls!
<u>FIVE</u>: G-Men!
<u>SIX</u>: Punks!
<u>SEVEN</u>: Goils!
<u>EIGHT</u>: Stooleys!
The COMPANY spin round on EIGHT and drill him with the single spoken word 'ZAP!'
<u>NINE</u>: Hey who's da looker?
The COMPANY spin back, their attention taken by the walk-across of MAE COUGHLIN in a spot
<u>ALL</u>: (Wolfwhistle)
<u>EIGHT</u>: Dat's da future Mrs Capone ... you're dead!
<u>GANGSTER</u> (Running in): Hey you screwballs better move. BIG AL's in town!
The COMPANY start to scramble as if eager to get out of the area, fights ensue which are halted in a freeze when CAPONE speaks. His entrance is a shock. AL is as he would have been in his mid twenties. He wears a suit and astrakhan coat.

AL Freeze! (The COMPANY freeze except that small parts of the body continue to quiver until AL shouts:-)
   Now! —
   Now hear dis alla you bums (to audience) and hear good
   Cos' dis is da story
   Da Pitch
   Da spiel dat has to be spieled
   Mei Capite (You understand everything?)
   You follow my Italian eh?
   Datsa good
       (He flicks his fingers and the COMPANY repeat subserviently 'Datsagood')
   Cos any punks now present, that find my story, aforementioned, difficult to stummick
       (ALL COMPANY zip out imaginary 38's and point them at the audience, they make clicking noises with their tongues)
   Die! (Click noise here)
   Go sleepy-byes!
   Fizzzzzzzz (AL makes the sound and demonstrates a fuse burning which explodes with a cymbal crash. The COMPANY slump forward as if dead)
   All right OK enough of the coytersies (courtesies) — we need polite introductions and explanatories
       (The COMPANY move quickly into new positions for the SPIEL)
AL: Name of hero!
ONE: (Company all kneel ONE stands) Mister Al 'Scarface' Capone The Four Deuces, South Wabash Avenue, Chicago City, Illinois
AL: Wisecrack!
TWO: (A pair form a comedy routine gag pair vaudeville style while others alter their places) Al Capone has just received a new simplified income tax form with only two sections (a) How much do you earn and
THREE: (b) send it!
       (there is a long pause — will CAPONE like it?)
AL: I like it!
COMPANY: He likes it!
AL: Standard alibi for hero
FOUR: We the jury find that Joe Howard (AL interrupts the speaker)
AL: the aforementioned (A stickler for phoney legal protocol)
FOUR: We, the jury, find that the afore-mentioned Joe Howard came to his death on the premises of 2300 South Wabash Avenue, from haemmorhage and shock (COMPANY take off hats in reverse) due to bullet wounds! (COMPANY put hats on)
AL: Innocent!
COMPANY: Not Guilty!
AL: General character reference for hero
FIVE: They was hard times
SIX: Deep Depression
SEVEN: Al was the victim and creation of his times
EIGHT: Al would come into the club with a bunch of boys (Two GANGSTERS close in). He was always a regular guy
NINE: Always courteous and quiet
TEN: Gave luverly funerals (AL clips head of TEN)

ELEVEN: Once when I work as a waiter in Joe Esposito's Bella Napoli Cafe he gave me a five dollar tip — justa for bringing him a cuppa coffe. He was a (CAPONE gives him a 5 dollar bill) Gooda guy!

ELEVEN: He was — a

COMPANY: All right!

> NEWSPANEL 2 ... A KIND KINDA GUY ... THE KINDA GUY THAT KILLS

SONG: 'KIND KINDA GUY'

COMPANY: ALL RIGHT ALL RIGHT ALL RIGHT!
ALL RIGHT ALL RIGHT
ALL RIGHT ALL RIGHT ALL RIGHT
AL CAPONE'S ALL RIGHT!

AL: HARD TIMES AND DEEP DEPRESSION WAS THE SCENE IN U.S.A.
(Company BUDDY CAN YOU SPARE A DIME? DESTITUTION DAY
dance) TIME FOR A MAN TO LIGHT A ROCKET
STICK COPS AND LAWYERS IN HIS POCKET
TIME FOR A KIND KINDA GUY

THE KINDA GUY THAT KILLS!

ZIP GUNS AND GANGSTER JUSTICE WAS ON THE MENU FOR THE DAY
SO SHUT YA MOUTH AND EAT YA DINNER, WHO SAYS THAT CRIME DON'T PAY?

TIME FOR A MAN WITH HOODLUM NOTIONS
TO SPRAY CHICAGO WITH BOOTLEG LOTION
TIME FOR A KIND KINDA GUY
THE KINDA GUY THAT KILLS!

ONE: (spoken) I swear to tell the truth

TWO: The distorted truth

THREE: And nothing but the distorted truth

COMPANY: So help us Al!

AL AND TWO GANGSTERS:	DA LITTLE GUYS GROW THIN	COMPANY:	KIND KINDA GUY
	DA BIGGER GUYS GROW FAT	(Sotto voce	KIND KINDA GUY
	COS DA LITTLE GUYS GET EATEN	with dance)	KIND KINDA GUY
	BY DA BIG GUYS DAT'S A FACT		HE'S DA KINDA GUY DAT KILLS.
	O.K. YOU'LL CONDEMN ME		HARD HARD HARD UP TIMES
	CALL ME LOUSY NO GOOD PUNK		HARD HARD HARD UP TIMES
	BUT REMEMBER WHERE YOU GOT DAT BOOZE		HARD HARD HARD UP TIMES
	AND GIVE DAT FACT SOME THUNK		YOU BET DEM TIMES WAS TOUGH TOUGH TOUGH!
	I PROVIDE DA SERVICE		BAD BAD BAD ABOOZE
	YOU SUPPLY DA NEED		BAD BAD BAD ABOOZE

AND IF YOU CANNOT PAY YOUR DUES
DEN NATURALLY YOU'LL BLEED

I STRUGGLED FROM DA GUTTER
I WON'T GO DERE NO MORE
AND ANY COP DAT PUTS ME DOWN
I'LL SPAGHETTI TO DA FLOOR
(gun spray)

BAD BAD BAD-A-BOOZE
IT'S DA BAD BOOZE ROTS
    YOUR GUTS. BOOZE BOOZE!
KIND KIND KINDA GUY
KIND KIND KINDA GUY
KIND KIND KINDA GUY
BANG! BANG!

AL & COMPANY: SMART DEALS AND PROHIBITION IS DA TRUE WAY TO SURVIVE
SO CLOSE YOUR TRAP AND USE YOUR MARBLES, DAT WAY YOU'LL STAY ALIVE.
TIME FOR A MAN WITH A RUBBER HOSE'LL
KEEP YOU COOL FOR HIS DISPOSAL
TIME FOR A KIND KINDA GUY
TIME FOR A KIND KINDA GUY
THE KINDA GUY THAT KILLS.
GA — BANG!
BANG!
(COMPANY Collapse or hold a freeze at the end of the number)

AL: O.K. I think you got the message. Nobody cross me in the next two hours cos I tend to get all confused up here (indicating his head) and then nasty things start happenin'. Right? Right. O.K. All you bums get offa da street while da clientele here present (signifying audience) and I have a short blab about my early connections. Move! (The COMPANY scatter off the playing area — They are scared). I apologise for da scum but they wasn't ever edjucated.

I feel it my duty — so that you may judge me fairly dat I fill you in with some small details of my early life. How my Momma and Poppa came to leave Italy, after sellin' up da spinach and spaghetti shop. My older brudders, Johnny and Frankie was around den and dey lived in a little seaside kinda place — not far from Napoli. Hey! Maybe you bums on da keyboard could rustle me up a slice of de old Neapolitan block (Soupy Italian music is played). Hey datsagood!

My brother Frankie was only a little kid then. You'd like to meet him?

<u>EXHIBIT TWO: 'IN THE BEGINNING'</u>

AL: Hey Frankie
FRANK CAPONI: You wanted me Al?
AL: Sure Frankie. Will you be so kind as to give dese palookas de old 'once upon a time' razzamatazz
FRANKIE: On the line Al. Once upon — (AL places his hand over the kid's mouth)
AL: I feel dat I should explain dat de reason I am not playing dis juvenile role is dat I don't do da juvenile voices so good, O.K? Continue kid.
FRANKIE: — a time the Caponi's lived in Castel Amara where my poppa used to run a grocery business and Momma used to take in washing
    (During this speech GABRIEL CAPONI enters with boxes and a sign 'CAPONI' listing goods for sale Vino (wine) Formaggio (cheese) Pomodori (Tomatoes) Gelato (Ice cream) etc.
    TERESA CAPONI enters and hangs washing line across the scaffold area to dry)
GABRIEL: (very softly) Teresa — Cara mia just for once forget the washing and help me with the shoppa — we've overslept again.
THERESA: (At top of her voice) Allright don't shouta so much. You wanna the people think we are not a happy family (ALL do a cod cheesy grin out to the audience and then back to normality). You wanna make more money — then let me get on with the washing and get Frankie to help you.

FRANKIE: (To audience) As you can see Momma has a slight speech problem — now and then she has to take a breath.
GABRIEL: (throwing cloth at Frankie) Hey Frank every day we start like this. There is work to be done — so come and help me with the shop eh? There's a gooda boy.
TERESA: (shouting) Then maybe your father won't shouta so much!
FRANKIE: Allright Allright I'm a coming (confidentially to audience) The reason they shout at me so much is that there is some doubt as to whether I am really a Caponi kid.
TERESA: (turning on him) Don't blame me — look at your Poppa. When he wheeled you out in the pram — I said when he came back — Gabriel! you crazy — that is not our kid!
GABRIEL: (shouts) O.K. (quietly) but it was a better pram!
 (THE CAPONIS busy themselves with setting up shop)
AL: (At pro arch lighting a cigar) I should at this juncture point out the fact that the Italian is by nature criminally inclined or as we say — a shrewd business man. And as business is about to start for the day I shall take this opportoonity to get me some udder rags on ready for the start of da story.
 (A COCK crows and the stage lightens with bright Italian sunshine, the COMPANY start to wake up opening imaginary windows, beating carpets, airing sheets, lovers part, arms stretch, faces yawn, chamberpots empty)
NEIGHBOUR 1: Buon Giorno!
NEIGHBOUR 2: Ciao
NEIGHBOUR 3: Hey it's a lovely day!
NEIGHBOUR 4: (looking up at the whore) Yea, If you only work at night (Altercation)
NEIGHBOUR 5: Hey Gabriel
GABRIEL: Si?
NEIGHBOUR 5: (enthusiastically) You know those tomatoes you sold me yesterday?
GABRIEL: Si
NEIGHBOUR 5: Lousy!
NEIGHBOUR 6: Hey Gina — You gotta my husband in there?
NEIGHBOUR 3: No! Your son (laughter)
NEIGHBOUR 6: Giorgio you hear me?
GIORGIO: No Momma (Face between whore's legs)
NEIGHBOUR 6: (sweetly) You get back home now and I promise faithfully — I will kill you!
NEIGHBOUR 7: Buon Giorno Gina — you fat cow
NEIGHBOUR 3: (Makes a well-known Italian Gesture)
NEIGHBOUR 8: Gabriel — delivered to the wrong door. It looka like the emigration visas you were talking about (He throws them down to the hands of GABRIEL)
GABRIEL: Mamma mia Teresa! They have come, the papers
TERESA: Che bella sorpressa! (what a surprise)
NEIGHBOUR 5: Good, if you're leaving we might get some decent tomatoes!
NEIGHBOUR 9: Visas for America? — hey who's the lucky one Caponi?

> NEWSPANEL... 1893 THE CAPONI DREAM...

NEIGHBOUR 10: You mad. Whata you want to go to crazy country for? They don't even speak Italian over there.
GABRIEL: Some bigga guy at the 'banca in Roma' told me that in America there is plenty big money to be made.
NEIGHBOUR 3: And plenty big men — Eh Teresa?
TERESA: No plenty big dollar, foul mouth. Maybe we can put some money in the kids pockets for once.
NEIGHBOUR 11: (Very excited to catch everyone's attention) Hey yesterday Fat Bandini told me something *fantastic* about America!
FRANKIE: Yea what? (agog)
NEIGHBOUR 11: (quickly) I don't know I've forgotten (crowd show disappointment)
TERESA: One thing — life is got to be betta in America

NEIGHBOUR 2: Si. Yesterday I said to the manager in the 'banca at Roma' — How do I stand for a loan and he says 'you don't Vanzetti — you kneel!'
GABRIEL: You see even little Italians have lost their pride.
ALL: That's right
FRANKIE: We go to America and live rich. Maybe buy a bigga car — eh Momma?
TERESA: Si
    (One of the COMPANY leaves the stage to change for LIBERTY)

    SONG AND DANCE 'GONNA BEND A NEW SHAPE'

TERESA/GABRIEL & FRANKIE:
WO-OH
OH LEAVE IT ALL BEHIND US
MAKE A NEW TOMORROW TODAY.

WO-OH
OH GO TO NEW YORK CITY
IN THE LAND OF U.S.A.
GONNA LEAVE THE LAND THAT WE KNOW
FOR A NEW ONE THAT WILL GROW
AND IF THE NEW WORLD
AIN'T THE SHAPE WE LIKE IT
WE'LL MAKE A NEW WORLD OF OUR OWN
AND IF THE NEW WORLD AIN'T
THE SHAPE WE LIKE IT
WE'LL MAKE A NEW WORLD
A NEW WORLD
A NEW WORLD OF OUR OWN.

COMPANY:
WO-OH
OH LEAVE IT ALL BEHIND YOU
MAKE A NEW TOMORROW, TODAY

WO-OH
OH GO TO NEW YORK CITY
IN THE LAND OF U.S.A.

TERESA/GABRIEL & FRANKIE:
GONNA GIVE THAT OLD DICE A THROW
FOR A NUMBER THAT WILL SHOW
THAT IF THE NEW WORLD
AIN'T THE SHAKE WE SHOOK IT
WE'LL SHAKE A NEW WORLD OF OUR OWN

COMPANY:
AND IF THE NEW WORLD AIN'T
THE SHAKE WE SHOOK IT
WE'LL SHAKE A NEW WORLD
A NEW WORLD
A NEW WORLD OF OUR OWN.

GOILS:
IF YOU CLOSE YOUR EYES YOU CAN NEARLY SEE IT
WHEN YOU FALL ASLEEP YOU CAN REALLY DREAM IT

MEN:
YOU ONLY DIE ONCE BUT YOU CAN LIVE TWICE
FOR ONCE IN YOUR LIFE TAKE YOUR OWN ADVICE

COMPANY:
AND DO IT
GET UP AND DO IT

MEN: GET ALL YOUR BAGS AND BUNDLES ABOARD
GOILS: MOVE THOSE LEGS. START WALKIN' TALL

COMPANY:	TO A NEW LIFE, THAT'S GOTTA BE BETTA BETTA-BETTA-BETTA-BETTA THERE'S GOTTA BE A BETTA WORLD. WO-OH OH GONNA TAKE A GAMBLE PUT A NICKEL IN THE FATE MACHINE WO-OH WATCH THAT PIN-BALL ROLLING LIGHT THAT MILLION DOLLAR STARR GONNA LEAVE THE LAND THAT WE KNOW FOR A NEW ONE THAT WILL GROW AND IF THE NEW WORLD AIN'T THE SHAPE WE LIKE IT WE'LL BEND A NEW SHAPE OF OUR OWN AND IF THE NEW WORLD AIN'T THE SHAPE WE LIKE IT WE'LL BEND A NEW WORLD A NEW WORLD A NEW WORLD OF OUR OWN.
REPRISE:	IF YOU CLOSE YOUR EYES YOU CAN NEARLY SEE IT to THERE'S GOTTA BE A BETTA WORLD.
REPRISE:	VERSE 3 ENDING . . . AND IF THE NEW WORLD AIN'T THE SHAPE WE LIKE IT WE'LL BEND A NEW WORLD YES WE'LL BEND A NEW WORLD YES WE'LL BEND A NEW WORLD OF OUR OWN!

The COMPANY drift off reprising slowly and very softly 'IF YOU CLOSE YOUR EYES etc.' We see three things (1) GABRIEL TERESA AND FRANKIE stage left in a tight protective group, they are apprehensive (2) LIBERTY appears on the central raised playing area and (3) the NEWSPANEL flickers message.

NEWSPANEL ... U.S.A. ELDORADO FOR IMMIGRANT ITALIANS ...

A spot picks out the GROUP, tired with battered cases and LIBERTY who holds a large flash torch inside an ice cream cornet and a 'furniture on credit' catalogue. She speaks with a broad Brooklyn accent and chews gum.

LIBERTY: Teresa and Gabriel Caponi you have now decided to leave your homeland, wishing to be numbered with the European poor in Brooklyn, New York. Welcome.
Let me show you the sights.
Over there is New York City (Sound cue of traffic noises),
Over there is New York Harbour (Sound cue; ships hooter).
And this — is — Brooklyn (Sound cue; shot and scream)
Kinda quaint — Huh?

EXHIBIT THREE 'THE IMMIGRANT'

TERESA: This is the Promised Land?
LIBERTY: Sure we promise you lots a things
 (Sung as a pledge)
 We promise that now you are an American Citizen
 You will from this moment on —
 Wards
 Be badly educated, badly housed and wait for it — badly paid.
 Gee. That must come as something of a disappointment —
 Buddy.
GABRIEL: Indeed — You see, sir
LIBERTY: Sir!!!!
TERESA: Pleasa forgive me
FRANKIE: Our English is notta so good
TERESA: Try harder Poppa
GABRIEL: Si (with great effort) Dear Sir — or Madam —
LIBERTY: That's better. Just don't take 'liberties' (She goofs audience)
TERESA: Look. What Poppa is trying to ask is where can we get apartment?
LIBERTY: Apartment? Immigrants? Look you just whisper in my ear how much megillah you got, then we'll have a good laff about it and start from there. O.K. Shoot.
GABRIEL: (Whispers his poverty through cornet held as an ear-trumpet) That much eh? (laughing at their ignorance) With that kinda money the place you're looking for is right over there. The Italian Quarter, Brooklyn. Welcome home.
  MUSIC: Reprise instrumental 'Bend a new shape' as spot comes up on tight GROUP OF IMMIGRANTS, they are trying to read, write, feed, work etc. within the area of the spot. It is cramped, they are filthy and shabby).
LIBERTY: (Taking them across) You'll find the accommodation a little cramped — Oh yea and you might need this — (hands them book) 'Furniture on credit' and this (handing them cornet torch) it tends to get dark even during the day in Brooklyn. Oh and another thing — don't buy insurance — just get a gun — got it?
  (THE CAPONIS stand bemused while LIBERTY removes halo and latches onto a passing GANGSTER)
LIBERTY: Hey, Buddy Can you spare a goil a Lucky?
GANGSTER: Sure thing baby. Say are you lookin' for a good time on the town?
LIBERTY: Am I? Do you know I've been stood here a long long time waitin' for just such an offer. Lead me to it.
GANGSTER: I'm leadin'
LIBERTY: (as they exit) Say are you married? (GANGSTER quickens his pace and off)
  (As the GANGSTER/LIBERTY exit, the CAPONIS walk across to the group of immigrants. As GABRIEL knocks three times on the edge of the spot circle it moves across three jerks as do the immigrants, the JANITOR pushes it back with three jerks and then opens imaginary door)
JANITOR: (A woman with a gruff voice) Whatdja want? You lookin' for somethin' — (an Overhead train shakes them to pieces) or somebody?
TERESA: We are lookin' for nice room. Clean with nice view.
JANITOR: This is Brooklyn lady. Things is different. That's why I talk like a guy. O.K?
TERESA: O.K. (deeply also)
JANITOR: I fix you up with a room — sharing. Four dollars a month. Two months in advance. (She snatches money from GABRIEL'S hand). No bath! No John! No Irish! Take it (Overhead train zooms past) or leave it.
GABRIEL: We take it!
JANITOR: (eyeing Teresa) Say lady, are you pregnant?
TERESA: Si!

JANITOR: Well take my advice, have it as quickly as possible and get it out to work!
TERESA: Si.
    MUSIC INCIDENTAL:
    (There is a spin off sound and the IMMIGRANTS disperse except for four who lift TERESA to shoulder level and AL moves in behind group. They place a white sheet over her body)
TERESA: Santa Maria (She is in labour and AL rolls out from behind group)
GABRIEL: It's girl!
AL: (revealed, he has a cigar in his mouth) Do me a favour!
GABRIEL: It's a boy!
TERESA: (As she is whirled off) Thank a heavens for that!
    (AL is kneeling upstage centre and GABRIEL stands over him, the lights dim or change colour. There is a moment)
GABRIEL: Kid. This is your Poppa speaking.
    Pretty soon I'm not gonna be here no more, so you betta listen good. Your Momma and I have decided to givea you the name Alphonso. O.K?
AL: O.K.
GABRIEL: O.K. And now you better start to do some growin' up kid.
    Things is a happening up here.

    NEWSPANEL: ... 1899 CAPONE BORN ... 'THE PROGRESSIVE ERA' ...

(Three POLITICIANS appear above AL on scaffold centre. As they speak each line they pull an imaginary puppet string which brings AL to life below them like Pinocchio)
(The POLITICIANS wear frock coats and top hats)
POLITICIAN A: One in every six wage earners unemployed (small pull raises right arm)
POLITICIAN B: Jobless men wander the country (small pull raises left arm)
POLITICIAN C: Two tablespoonfuls of bourbon and honey (head and body)
POLITICIAN A: Continuous streams of immigrants flood the market (onto right foot)
POLITICIAN B: Growth of unskilled labour outruns the demand (onto left foot)
POLITICIAN C: One glass of sasafrass (upright stance)
POLITICIAN A: Hang all Molly McGuires (lunge right)
POLITICIAN B: 24,000 strikes between '81 and 1900 (lunge left)
POLITICIAN C: Labour disputes will lead to violence
ALL: BUY BANDAGES NOW! (spin circle to face politicians)
AL: Hey what about some protection for me?

    SONG AND MARCH/DANCE 'MUCKRAKERS MARCH'

AL & COMPANY:
CONCILIATION-ARBITRATION
ARE JUST AROUND THE BEND
PROTECTION FOR THE IMMIGRANT
SOCIAL EVILS SOON WILL END

THIS IS THE 'PROGRESSIVE ERA', AL
GOOD MEN WILL FIGHT AND WRITE
EXPOSING GRAFT AND CORRUPTION
PUTTING ALL THESE WRONGS TO RIGHT.

SO REMEMBER, KID, THAT AS YOU GROW
AND BUMS LIKE YOU MAY FAIL
THAT BRIGHT STAR CALLED T. ROOSEVELT
WILL ENSURE THAT TRUTH PREVAILS

(COMPANY sing sotto voce staccato under song — Then reprise all three verses loudly a culminating march in the grand manner)

(Silver top hats and silver lapelled tail-coats with tights and canes)

  REPEAT:
(At the end of the SONG, the three POLITICIANS are holding the stars and stripes before them)

POLITICIAN A: Hey Al, can you handle yourself?
AL: Sure watch this (AL knocks down all the COMPANY to a freeze with four timed punches)
POLITICIAN A: Well you betta move — There's a job as waiter and bouncer at Frank Yale's Cabaret Club and you better be smart. He's one of Johnny Torrio's torpedoes.
AL: Who's he?
POLITICIAN A: You'll find out soon enough (to COMPANY) O.K. Move!
(The COMPANY disperse)
AL: (To audience) O.K. If I gotta woik, I gotta woik. But I ain't creepin' like dose udder immigrant bums. I got it all woicked out see.
O.K. Gimme da disguise bit (A COMPANY MEMBER helps him into an old coat, puts on a bowler, gives him a bendy cane, AL pulls false moustache and red nose on elastic round his top lip. He is CHARLIE CHAPLIN). You like it eh? Who says Italians have only got spaghetti for brains? O.K. Bring on da jobs!

EXHIBIT FOUR 'THE FIRST JOB'

The next scene is done in the style of a silent movie and the sequence of events and business are to be found in the stage notes. We see AL walking towards four separate doors each offering a job (1) 'On the waterfront' (2) 'Police recruit' (3) 'Bank Clerk' and (4) 'Dishwasher/Waiter at Frank Yale's Cabaret Club'. As AL approaches each of the doors he is brushed aside — the sequence of events being narrated by the FILM DIRECTOR: Speaking through megaphone.

DIRECTOR: (in plus fours with peak cap back to front)
It's Spaghetti Al (AL pulls a face at the DIRECTOR)
Ooops we don't like that kinda Italian Leera. Get it folks!
Well here's Al after his first job. How's he gonna get on?
(WATER FRONT BULLY pushes Al to one side as he opens the door)
— Oh Oh Poor Al didn't expect that kind of dock hand
Maybe there's better luck at the Cop Shop
(KEYSTONE COP pushes him aside) Hey has the world gone crazy?
Life is supposed to be Fun Fun Fun!
Hey Al how about a job at the bank? Get those lil' ole grease-ball fingers on those lovely greenbacks
(BANK MANAGER pushes him down) Hey! Who ya pushin' mister?
Why don't you try your luck in show biz Al?
(NATTY FRANK YALE pushes aside) Poor old Al, he's not gonna write any pages in our golden history today.
But don't go away folks. Just sit back and laff along with 'Al and Pals' in the Essanay Company's latest smasheroo called 'Stony Broke Blues'. Take it away Frank!
LIGHTS come up on the figure of NATTY FRANK YALE and the OBEE DOBEE GOILS)
This is set on the raised area. FRANK with two goils centre and goils on each of the other four platforms

NEWSPANEL ... CONEY ISLAND FRANK YALE'S DINKY DOOBEES ...

SONG: STONY BROKE BLUES

FRANK: POOR LITTLE AL   (GIRLS dance)
       LIKE SIMPLE SIMON
       HASN'T GOTTA PENNY
       FOR A PIE   DOOBEE GOILS: NO PIE
       POOR LITTLE AL
       NO LUCK IN HIS LOCKET
       HE'S GOTTA GET A JOB
       OR DIE   DOOBEE GOILS: DON'T CRY

	COS HE'S		
	STONY BROKE	DOOBEE GOILS:	OOO-AH
	WALKING THE STREETS ALL DAY		DINKY DOO-BEE-BOO-BEE
	STONY BROKE		OO-AH
	BEGS FOR A DIME A DAY		DINKY DOO-BEE-DOO-BEE
ALL:	WHEN HE STROLLS DOWN TO THE METROPOLE		
	HE'S GOT NO SHOES ON HIS FEET		
	JUST LIKE THOSE LINES OF INFINITY		
	HE CAN'T MAKE BOTH ENDS MEET		
FRANK:	STONY BROKE	DOOBEES:	OOO-AH
	BABY, WE'RE TELLIN' YOU	DOOBEES:	DINKY DOO-BEE-DOO-BEE
	STONY BROKE	DOOBEES:	OOO-AH
ALL:	BABY IT'S HELL		
	WHEN YOU'RE STONEY BROKE		
	IT'S PLAIN TO SEE		
	HE'S GOT THOSE STONY BROKE BLUES.		

(Silent movie commences in front of Stoney Broke Singers)

FRANK: POOR LIL AL
GOTTA DINE ON GARBAGE
THE PREACHER CALLS THEM
WAGES OF BIN   DOOBEES: SIN!
POOR LIL AL
HIS PLASTER IS PEELING
THE PAPER DOWN HIS TROUSERS
IS THIN   DOOBEES: SO THIN
COS HE'S DOWN AND OUT   DOOBEES: OO-AAH
BUMMING A BEER EACH DAY   HICKY DOO-BEE-DOO-BEE
DOWN AND OUT   OOO-AH
DROWNS ALL THE BLUES THAT WAY   HICKY DOO-BEE-DOO-BEE

ALL: WASHING DISHES DOWN ON FORTY NINTH
HANDS ALL WRINKLED AND SORE
JUST LIKE LITTLE RED RIDING HOOD
HE CAN'T KEEP THE WOLF FROM THE DOOR.

FRANK: DOWN AND OUT   DOOBEES: OOO-AAH
BABY WE'RE TELLING YOU   OOO-BEE-DOO-BEE-DOO-BEE
DOWN AND OUT   OOO-AH

ALL: BABY IT'S HELL
WHEN YOU'RE
STONY BROKE
IT'S PLAIN TO SEE
HE'S GOT THOSE
STONY BROKE BLUES.

FRANK: POOR LIL AL
EVERYBODY SHOVES HIM
BUT SOON HE'LL DO THE SHOVIN'
HIMSELF   DOOBEES: WHAM
POOR LIL AL
EVERYBODY SNUBS HIM
BUT SOON HE'LL RUB THOSE
SNUBBERS OUT   DOOBEES: EERASE

	COS HE'S ON THE MAKE		OO-AAH
	BIDING HIS TIME EACH DAY		TICKY DOO-BEE-DOO-BEE
	ON THE TAKE		OO-AAH
	THE FINDERS-KEEPERS WAY		TOCKY DOO-BEE-DOO-BEE
<u>ALL</u>:	WEARING SUITS SO FLASHY AND RITZY		
	DIAMOND TIE-PINS AS WELL		
	THOSE DIMES MAY SEEM ITZY-BITZY		
	BUT ITZY-BITZY DIMES CAN SWELL		
<u>FRANK</u>:	ON THE MAKE	<u>DOOBEES</u>:	OO-AAH
	BABY WE'RE TELLING YOU		OO-BEE-DOO-BEE-DOO-BEE
	ON THE TAKE		OO-AAH
	BABY IT'S SWELL		
	WHEN YOU'RE ON THE TAKE		
	IT'S PLAIN TO SEE		
	GOT NO STONY BROKE		
	AIN'T NO PHONEY JOKE		
	GOT NO STONY BROKE		
	BLUE-BLUE		
	BLUEDY		
	BLUES! (money bag into hat when siren sounds)		

(The 'OLD TIME MOVIE SEQUENCE commences at the beginning of the second verse and the bag of money should fall into AL's hat on the final word Blues)

<u>SILENT MOVIE BUSINESS</u> (To be performed at triple speed)

A director speaks as a Camera crew in a trolley shoot the sequence of the silent film. AL in Chaplin dress turns and runs in slow motion towards DOOR ONE which comes downstage towards him and the audience. He knocks and it opens to reveal a typical Mack Sennet bully (the door is marked WATERFRONT WORKER REQUIRED Apply within). The BULLY pushes Al to one side and the DOOR 1 moves across stage right and DOOR TWO come s down. It is marked POLICE STATION Recruits required). A knock and a KEYSTONE COP hits Al with truncheon as DOOR TWO crosses to stage left. DOOR THREE comes down marked BANK OF AMERICA Bank Clerk required). Al knocks and a fat BANK MANAGER pushes him in face and the door floats off stage right. DOOR FOUR comes down marked CONEY ISLAND CABARET CLUB. Al knocks and NATTY FRANK YALE punches him in stomach and Al sits with a bump on the floor while the four doors shunt into the following stage positions. The POLICE STATION goes at an angle stage right, the BANK OF AMERICA at an angle stage left while the CABARET and WATERFRONT doors reverse to display on the opposite side the interior design of the CABARET RESTAURANT.
At the end of the second verse of STONEY BROKE BLUES the following sequence takes place. Two restaurant tables with checked cloths are placed stage left and right downstage with two chairs at one table and one at the other.
Al stands outside restaurant. He is broke (all this done in dumb show). Empty pockets.
Al sees a string hanging out of his top pocket, he pulls it and reveals a sausage.
Al takes salt out of side pocket, seasons sausage and is about to devour it when COOGAN KID AND SCRAPS THE DOG enter. They are starving. Can you spare us some food?
Al shares food with them and they are about to eat when
FAT BANK MANAGER holding large bag of money accompanied by KEYSTONE COP pushes AL and the KID roughly to one side. They disappear into the Bank but not before Al trips up BANK MANAGER with his cane and SCRAPS bites the policeman's bum.
AL, KID & SCRAPS run and hide at side of restaurant as PRETTY WAITRESS enters. It is in fact MAE COUGHLIN.
HEAD WAITER (the BULLY from the waterfront) enters and slaps the girl around. Work harder!

MAE lays up the table. She puts flowers into a small vase.
AL enters while the Kid keeps a look-out. Al takes the flowers while she is not looking.
AL offers her his bouquet. She accepts. He tickles her under the chin. Pinches a kiss.
MAE is coy but spots the BULLY who enters and is about to lambast AL, who produces a note/card
clearly saying 'Waiter needed'. He points to himself. Feel my muscles.
BULLY accepts him, supplies an apron and shows him what is required.
BANK MANAGER AND WIFE enter and BULLY crosses to show them to their seats.
AL at that precise time is going to offer MAE one of the seats as a gallant gesture.
There is at this point a piece of chair business where they each offer the chair to another, then it is
removed by second person just as the chair is about to be sat on. Each hits the floor and stays there
in this sequence. WIFE has chair snatched by MAE who places it for herself, it is snatched from beneath
her by the BANK MANAGER, it is snatched from beneath him by AL, it is snatched from beneath him
by BULLY but as the BULLY is finally about to sit on the chair the prostrate AL pushes it from
underneath him with his foot.
AL leaps up and he is chased by the BULLY, BANK MANAGER, HIS WIFE round the stage.
MAE runs to POLICE STATION DOOR and opens it and as the chasing group go towards it
AL assisted by KID and SCRAPS kicks them all up the bum and they shoot through the door. AL
produces huge key and locks them up.
At that precise moment the KEYSTONE COP exits from BANK holding the money.
AL shoots the COP and the money flies up in the air and is caught by AL in his bowler hat. As it is
caught, AL, MAE, KID and SCRAPS are in a freeze. The money bag should drop into the hat on the
very last note of STONY BROKE BLUES.
The whole sequence is done at a very fast silent movie speed and all the hits and bumps as well as objects
falling or bags flying through the air should be accompanied by whees, whistles, horns, rim shots and
cymbal crashes.
It appears complicated at first but if taken piecemeal soon becomes a very funny and satisfying business.

EXHIBIT FIVE: CUPIDS BOW

NEWSPANEL ... AL MEETS MAE COUGHLIN ...

(At the end of STONY BROKE BLUES :— Al is divested of his CHAPLIN costume and he talks to the audience)

AL: (to audience) O.K. So it ain't much of a job — but Coney Island is the kinda place you meet people. People that matter, People that ......

(MAE COUGHLIN standing in the shadow of the raised area whistles)

AL: Who is that? Who is dat dere?

MAE: It's me

AL: Hello me. How are ya?

MAE: Me? Oh I'm fine. How are you?

AL: I'm fine too — Hey you're the kid that was working as a waitress at the cabaret club — Say why don't you come down here a minute?

MAE: Why?

AL: Why do you keep on asking questions?

MAE: I do?

AL: You just done it again. Look I wanted you to come down here (she is suddenly right in front of him) because I wanted to say — er — I wanted to say (thinking of something) How much I like your dress kid.

(They both look down at the dress quickly and up again, they are very close)

MAE: (brightly) You do?

AL: Sure

MAE: I bought it all by myself

AL: A career girl too (to the audience)

MAE: You're laffing at me (hurt)
AL: No I really think it's nice — it's some container (To the band sotto voce) You creeps on the keyboard give me some of that romantica (they play) — datsagood. You know we should get more acquainted — closer. You see under this cold hard exterior —
MAE: Beats a cold hard heart?
AL: Hey knock it off — whose laffin' at who now? (He slides an arm round the back of her but doesn't touch her)
MAE: (freezes) Please! Don't touch my body!
AL: But I want to!
MAE: O.K. — Just a little
AL: (He touches and slides his hand down her, she goes dreamy) You see it didn't hoit kid. Don't freeze up on me. Relax. Life is for livin' you know. I wasn't plannin' on no major exploration. I just wanted to say . . . . . .
MAE: (feeding him the right words) You're pretty?
AL: You're pretty and . . .
MAE: Different?
AL: That you're pretty and different and . . .
MAE: Irish?
AL: Yea, that you're pretty and different and . . . IRISH!
(There is a sudden explosion of action with an IRISH JIG played very quickly as members of O'Hara's gang from the Irish quarter of New York enter. They have green hat bands and green ties with matching pocket handkerchiefs. They have encircled AL and pushed MAE against the pro arch. There is a .45 up AL's nose).
RYAN O'HARA: Allow us to introduce ourselves little one — we are the darlin' children of Big Daddy O'Hara from the Hazy Dazy on 9th Brooklyn*. I am Ryan, myself and this is me tiny brudder Smilin Boy O'Hara (there is absolutely no flicker of a smile on his face)
AL: (looks up at him) He's smilin'? He looks more like a bulldog!
RYAN O'HARA: Sure. The reason being that chasing after a little Italian feller like yourself he ran face first into a brick wall . . . and when Big Daddy found out that he'd been sleepin' around wid de little Italian's wife — he had his teeth pulled out!* He is what you might call a naughty boy.
   * GANGSTERS say here: 'DATSARIGHT!'
GANGSTERS: Tut tut tut tut
MAE: We was only talking, Ryan
GANGSTERS: (roused like lions) Grrrrrr!
AL: And I touched her a little
GANGSTERS: (really wild) Garowwwwrrrrrr!!!!
AL: That was wrong huh?
RYAN O'HARA: Very wrong little one. A mistake. An error of the judgement. Cos although we are Cattolicks, we don't like Cattolicks dat are Greaseballs! . . .
GANSTER STIFF: Wops!
GANGSTER SQUIRT: Dagos!
GANGSTER GOOFBALL: Spaghetti Creeps!
RYAN O'HARA: Messin' around wid our girls — especially when dey are called (they all whip their guns round onto MAE)
MAE: Mae Coughlin (nervous)
RYAN O'HARA: Mae Coughlin (whipping guns back on AL)
MAE: Ryan. Please give him a chance — he wasn't doin' no harm
RYAN O'HARA: I'll tell you what, kid. We are sweet law abiding citizens . . .

GANGSTERS: Citizens!
RYAN O'HARA: ... and to protect society from punks like you we would normally knock you off and we all have licences for our mouthorgans, (they ALL produce them for AL's hurried scrutiny) but as we do not like to leave bodies lyin' about all over da streets, we will give you a break. Here is a 'C' note (BULLDOG thrusts it into his mouth). You get yourself out of town and there will be less infection in the air of New York
GANGSTERS: New York!
AL: Is that your message?
RYAN O'HARA: That is the note of instruction, kid
AL: Well I gotta message for Big Daddy O'Hara
RYAN O'HARA: He's got a message (The GANGSTERS CORPSE). Lay it on me creep!
AL: Well it's short, Italian and it goes something like this
 (AL turns on each of them and delivers a series of individual knockout blows. The O'HARA'S should finish up, on and under things. Very quick and funny)
AL: (To audience) You see what I mean about people upsettin' me!
 (to MAE with incredible gentleness) Sorry baby, where were we?
MAE: You were touchin' me — just a little
AL: Thatsaright. So I was
MAE: Maybe I could help some this time (She kisses him very carefully almost shyly — he does not react) You don't have to kiss me back
AL: (taking her hand) I know that — er — Mae
MAE: Mae Coughlin
AL: I know that Mae Coughlin, but the Italians are like the Irish — great gamblers (AL spins her into him like something he would learn at a Valentino dance school. They kiss)
MAE: Well Al, do you think you dealt yourself a good hand?
AL: Sure kid — hence the royal flush (He suddenly sweeps her up into his arms
 I like you Mae and I'd like to see you again tonight.
MAE: (looking at the GANGSTERS that are just coming to and slinking off) Are you sure that'll be safe?
AL: Yea, it'll be safe. I think they got the right message (Still holding her in his arms) NOBODY TOLD YOU TO LEAVE!
GANGSTERS: NO SIR! (They all freeze)
MAE: (very softly) Tonight then? .
AL: Sure — Say where shall I find you?
MAE: You'll find me at the PINK PINEAPPLE SPEAKEASY Soft Drink Parlour on Second Avenue
AL: Sounds interestin' What happens there?
MAE: (Tongue in cheek) Er it's a centre for POETRY READING AND PHILOSOPHICAL DISCUSSION (Al drops her like a sack of coal unceremoniously and walks away)
AL: I don't think I've drunk that kind of stuff before. (To GANGSTERS) Hey you heavies had better move — tell your boss that Al Capone — dats spelt T-R-O-U-B-L-E don't like being muscled. NOW MOVE!
GANGSTER: YESSIR (they cut off)
MAE: I'll see you later Al.
AL: Sure thing baby (She goes but he stops her with) Hey — maybe we could do a little more of that touchin'! O.K.?
MAE: O.K. Ciao
 The stage is empty as AL comes down to speak to the audience but during the speech we are aware of the presence of JOHNNY TORRIO, he is a man in his late middle years, immaculately dressed in grey overcoat and homburg. He resembles more an executive or County Planning Officer than a full-time killer and 'booze king')

AL: Sometimes you can classify a broad as a looker or a non looker. That I like this one and I don't like that one. Then, suddenly, you see one who is completely different from all da others and dats the one ya gotta have. You know da feelin'? — I think I have found myself such a sweet potatoe.

EXHIBIT SIX TORRIO'S NIGHT SCHOOL

TORRIO: (calm, smooth of tongue, adroit in manner) Sweet Potatoe is da word. I've a been watching you Al.
AL: Who is dis bum?
TORRIO: (unruffled) You're a gooda boy. You move well. Growing up fast. Maybe I could use you somewhere in the city.
AL: Oh yea. Who are you?
(TORRIO'S TORPEDOES AND GOLDIE KANDINSKI his MOLL enter)
TORRIO: (with a sardonic laugh) Torrio. Johnny Torrio, I own the city of New York
AL: Well look Torrero, you got the wrong bull-calf. O.K.?
(AL turns and walks off but is picked up and walked back by the TORPEDOES)
TORRIO: (As if AL is a little boy) Al. Al. You calla me MR Torrio or MR Torrio, SIR. I prefer that
AL: My name is Al Capone and the only person I ever called 'sir' was my poppa
TORRIO: Thatsa allright Al (to BAND) Hey punks give me some blood-freezing music O.K.? (They play 'Dance of the Sugar Plum Fairies' — There is a double take). Now. You just need a little helping — some small instruction in social manners. Would you believe it — Goldilocks here was once a dumb broad.
GOLDILOCKS: (Dumb as hell) Yea datsright already. (She chews continuously)
TORRIO: Shuddup (Her face shuts)
So Al, here is your foist lesson
(The TORPEDOES hold him half nelsons)
AL: Hey what is dis?
TORRIO: (As an instruction) Good evening — Al
(No response, TORRIO signals to GOLDIE who holds her handbag in front of his balls and belts it, AL collapses)
AL: Ooo! — (learning fast) Good evening Mr Torrio
TORRIO: Sir?
(No response, GOLDIE repeats the medicine)
AL: Ooo! Sir!
TORRIO: (coming to AL) Yes. I like the little flourish at the end. Bravo. You learna fast. (He puts his arm round him) I like you. You're a clever boy. How would you like to work for me eh?
AL: I would deem that a great privilege Mr Torrio (ALL look at him, there is a tense moment) Sir (relief all round). Just tell me what I have to do and I'll do it.
TORRIO: No rush. No rush. Calm down kid. You like a crazy hot chestnut. My boys will explain your work (He pushes AL across to the heavies)
TORPEDOE ONE: You do 'small soivices' for people
TORPEDOE TWO: Put a squeeze on all bums that do not support the Torrio/Brooklyn Missionary Fund
GOLDIE: Arrange little axe-aye-dental rub-outs. Mean Deeds! (She kisses him)
TORRIO: Shuddup.
Al you just keep things quiet for me — on the avenues, at the clubs, at voting time. Do a little leaning — a little pushing. Generally tidy up for me. What do you say?
AL: I'm ready to woik for you Mr Torrio, Sir
TORRIO: Good
(THE TORPEDOES, GOLDIE and AL turn at attention to face the NEWSPANEL, there is quasi empire-building music played incidentally as they watch the message)
TORRIO: You are now a member of the Torrio Organisation and will move into my territory as part of The Five Pointers Gang

NEWSPANEL ... JOHN TORRIO'S 5 POINTERS GANG TERRORIZE NEW YORK

(This music changes into vaudeville knockabout comedian music and all the characters change their hats and faces to represent red-nosed comics, they form and re-form funny groups on each burst of music)

TORPEDOE ONE: Al Capone you have now entered the world ...
TORPEDOE TWO: ... of the professional gangster
TORPEDOE ONE: Here is your first 'G' (Stuffs note in top pocket)
TORPEDOES: Start learning your lessons well
(MUSIC burst)
TORRIO: Al I understand that you did a short stretch in the army before the Coney Island job. Is that right?
AL: Sure and I loined two things
TORPEDOES: He loined two things!
GOLDIE: What was that Al?
AL: The way IN and the way OUT!
GOLDIE: Crazy for knowledge!
(MUSIC burst)
TORRIO: Nothing else of use Al?
AL: Sure I loined that a guy wid a machine gun can fuzz out fifty bums with .45's
GOLDIE: Hey I got an idea!
TORPEDOES: She's got an idea!
TORRIO: Shuddup. (Back to normal and the torpedoes exit) Al I got an idea. Although I liked the way you handled the Irish problem just now. I still think you need a little tuition, refinement, before I can put my ideas into practice. We must erase some of the small crudities that still adhere. Remember Al — there are two kindsa people. Those that 'watch' and those that 'do'.
AL: What do you want me to do?
TORRIO: Watch
GOLDIE: Watch and ... listen, kid.
Respect is what you must command
TORRIO: So that no kind of horse manure (He signals GOLDIE to kneel) will ever shoot you crap.
AL: Instruct me on how to acquire this respect, so that life can be a bed of roses and I can reap the benefits.
TORRIO: Certainly kid. First you gotta get ...

SONG: 'A LITTLE KNUCKLE KNOWLEDGE'

TORRIO/GOLDIE: A LITTLE KNUCKLE KNOWLEDGE TO SEE YOU THROUGH KID
A LITTLE KNUCKLE KNOWLEDGE TO GET YOU BY
YOU WON'T NEED CLEVER ALPHABETS
OR BOOKS ON 'HOW AND WHY'
JUST A LITTLE SIMPLE ARITHMETIC
TO COUNT KNUCKLES ONE TO FIVE
COS YOU'LL NEVER GET ANY TRUCKLE WHERE THERE'S KNUCKLE
YEA, A LITTLE KNUCKLE KNOWLEDGE WILL GET YOU BY

(a group of DANCING BOXERS enter and join the PRINCIPALS)

TORRIO/AL: A LITTLE KNUCKLE KNOWLEDGE TO SEE YOU THROUGH KID
GOLDIE & A LITTLE KNUCKLE KNOWLEDGE TO GET YOU BY
BOXERS: YOU WON'T NEED DEMPSEY'S EXPERTISE
TO BUST THOSE FINKS UP WIDE
JUST A LITTLE SIMPLE SURGERY
WITH A THOMPSON OR FORTY-FIVE

>   COS YOU'LL NEVER GET ANY SCHMUCKLE WHERE THERE'S
>   KNUCKLE
>   YEA A LITTLE KNUCKLE KNOWLEDGE WILL GET YOU BY

TORRIO: (spoken) Learn these lessons well, thru and true, so that no kind of vermin steals cheese from the traps what you have set.
AL: To do this I need to be well-groomed. The guy that starts favourite on the race-track of life
TORRIO: In short, Al, you've gotta have a certain 'savoir faire'
AL: Huh?
TORRIO: That is French Al — it means bull-shit, O.K.?
     (A group of DANCING DUMBELLES who will dress and groom AL)

AL & DUMBELLES:	A LITTLE SNAPPY DRESSING TO SEE YOU THROUGH KID A LITTLE SNAPPY DRESSING TO GET YOU KNOWN YOU WON'T NEED DIRTY WORKING CLOTHES OR SUITS DAT AIN'T HAND SEWN BUT THIS BEAUTIFUL PAIR OF PIN-STRIPED PANTS AND A TIE AND SHOES TWO-TONE COS YOU'LL ALWAYS FEEL FLASH-HAPPY WHEN YOU'RE SNAPPY YEA A LITTLE SNAPPY DRESSING WILL GET YOU KNOWN
	A LITTLE SNAPPY DRESSING TO SEE YOU THROUGH KID A LITTLE SNAPPY DRESSING WILL GET YOU SET YOU WON'T WEAR ANY HAND-ME-DOWNS OF SISTER'S SECOND BEST BUT A CAMEL COLOURED FEDORA (This is put on) TO GO WITH YOUR MATCHING VEST (on goes coat) COS YOU'LL ALWAYS FEEL SO DANDY WHEN YOU'RE SNAPPY YES A LITTLE SNAPPY DRESSING WILL GET YOU SET

TORRIO: Finally Al, you gotta be seen with the right people
AL: So no one takes advantage of me?
TORRIO: You need a strong right arm to guard you during the day
AL: And a sweet potatoe to sleep on at night
TORRIO: Exactly — Don't get into tussles unless you got muscle and when you're alone and can't be seen —
AL: Then take a tumble with da crepe da chine!
TORRIO: You got it!
     (A GANGSTER GORILLA and a BROAD with KNOCKERS enter and lead Al arm in arm down the stage)

AL & COMPANY:	A LITTLE TIT AND MUSCLE TO SEE YOU THROUGH KID A LITTLE TIT AND MUSCLE WILL MAKE YOU SWELL
GORILLA:	YOU WON'T NEED ANY STUMBLE-BUMS
BROAD:	OR BROADS WITH BRAINS AS WELL
GORILLA:	JUST A TORPEDOE WHO CAN USE A GUN
BROAD:	AND A DOLL WHO RINGS YOUR BELL
COMPANY:	OOOO! COS YOU'LL NEVER GET HIT OR GUZZLED WHEN THERE'S MUZZLE YEA A LITTLE TIT AND MUSCLE WILL MAKE YOU LITTLE TIT AND MUSCLE WILL MAKE YOU LITTLE TIT AND MUSCLE WILL MAKE YOU
AL: Shouts:	(Bang, bang, bang, bang, bang, bang, bang!) YEA. A LITTLE TIT AND MUSCLE WILL MAKE YOU SWELL! WOOO!

BLACK OUT

EXHIBIT SEVEN 'OUTSIDE THE PINK PINEAPPLE SPEAKEASY'

The COMPANY and PRINCIPALS exit and three reading lecterns are set, they carry slogans like 'Enlightenment' 'Culture' etc. Behind each lectern stands a GANGSTER and downstage right of them a CULTURAL CREEPESS. She wears all the trappings of a do-gooder — a life member of the Townswomen's Guild. She has glasses on a necklace hanging and a poetry book in her hand. She is gushing, extrovert and funny, when she moves we get the impression that her body goes first and then the head trails afterwards like a trailing fox-fur)

CULTURAL CREEPESS: The city has many attractions
But think of its vices and sins
When once in the vortex of fasion
How soon the course downwards begins!

That's what our fathers used to say to us here in New York and on the western farms — but did we heed its message? (No interest from GANGSTERS)

CULTURAL CREEPESS: (Louder) But did we HEED its message?

GANGSTERS: (coming to) No Sir!

CULTURAL CREEPESS: No sir. Indeed we did not — so maybe we will listen now. Maybe the scales will fall from our ears and our eyes hear the message of the New Social Gospel. Maybe here at your local soft drinks parlour where the mind and body (She strokes her own) are not fuzzled and be-muzzled by the demon drink. Maybe here you will learn through our testimony and verse the true message for the future prosperity of the United States and its people. (To GANGSTERS — out of the side of her mouth and still smiling) Smile you bums

SUNG:	WELCOME ALL TO OUR HUMBLE SOCIAL CENTRE
GANGSTERS:	CENTRE
CREEPESS:	WHERE YOU CAN HELP TO FIGHT THE EVIL TEMPTER
GANGSTERS:	TEMPTER
CREEPESS:	WITH HYMNS AND WORDS AND VERSE YOU'LL GET ON TOP
GANGSTERS:	GET ON TOP
CREEPESS:	LOSE SATAN IN BAD WHISKY AND FIND GOD IN SODA-POP
GANGSTERS:	SODA-POP!

CULTURAL CREEPESS: Welcome all to the P.P.P.R.C.D.C. The Pink Pineapple Poetry Reading and Cultural Discussion Centre. Where we hope (Putting on glasses and looking earnest) through the poetry of this country's great literary giants to formulate new social and political doctrines for a nation whose wealth and power has apparently outstripped (She feels her body) — its ability to cope with the problems that this wealth has brought. The simple values that have been complicated by evils like injustice (GANGSTERS Look off R) graft (They look off L) Police Corruption (They look behind lecterns) and Bootleg Booze!

GANGSTERS: (very enthusiastically) Yea!

CULTURAL CREEPESS: (smiling) Take your hats off you creeps
So tonight we extend to you a very special welcome. For we have with us three new converts to our cause. Meet Gino Gyp the Blood

GINO GYP THE BLOOD: How are ya

CULTURAL CREEPESS: Lefty Louie

LEFTY LOUIE: Nice to meet ya

CULTURAL CREEPESS: And Florida . . . J. Sugar-Candy?

FLORIDA: Hi there (They all look at him — he shrugs his shoulders)

CULTURAL CREEPESS: Now Gino, tell us, what are you going to read for us this evening?

GINO GYP THE BLOOD: (In exaggerrated Brooklyn Accent) 'Contentment' by Oliver Wendell Holmes

CULTURAL CREEPESS: Wonderful. Ladies and Gentlemen some lines from one of America's truly great men. Take it away boys

GINO GYP THE BLOOD: (Receiving book from CREEPESS)

'Contentment' by oliver handle wendell, womble handle wimble (clearing throat)
Contentment . . .
   Little I ask, my wants are few
   I only wish a hut of stone
LEFTY LOUIE: (received book from CREEPESS upside down)
   One a such is hand at close And
   (She turns it up the correct way)
   And close at hand is such a one
   In yonder street that fronts the sun (He points dramatically off)
FLORIDA: (Receiving book from CREEPESS)
   A little place for you and me
   To spend our lives in liber
   (She turns over a single page)
   Ty!
   SUNG: Amen
CULTURAL CREEPESS: Thank you, thank you gentlemen for that truly moving moment. Three bright lights shine through the murk of New York City and talking of bright lights — look who we have here (enter drunk OFFICER O'FLAHERTY) Ever vigilant for our well-being and safety, our own Officer O'Flaherty. Applause please for this noble champion of right and justice. Officer will you join our happy band for some verse and vanilla fizz?
OFFICER O'FLAHERTY: Not me buddy, I shall be takin' meself along the darlin' streets of Little Italy here and who knows but I don't think that I shall be passin' this way again until 6 a.m. If you'se get me meaning (Gives large and knowing wink)
CULTURAL CREEPESS: Of course we do friend . . . May God be with you and guide your boots carefully along the straight path of law and order (SHE slips him a wad of notes) And now as you won't be troubling us until the early morning — we can get down to main event of the evening (The GANGSTERS lift O'Flaherty at the elbow so he exits walking on air) which is to welcome one and all to the PINK PINEAPPLE SPEAKEASY!
   (LIGHTS change. The GANGSTERS circus the lecterns to reveal three dreadful pink and silver pineapples in front of which are placed tables and chairs. All the COMPANY are drinking champagne while the CREEPESS has ripped off top coat to reveal floozie twenties dress. A TRUCK enters stage left behind which is BIG DIAMOND JIM COLOSIMO. The truck acts as a small night club stage and an outlet for BIG JIM and customers. The atmosphere is one of licentious cruelty. Artificially titivating. Sitting on the table stage right is the pineapple's COMPERE — LILY LUSH. All are drinking from bottles and smoking cigarette holders.

NEWSPANEL . . . 17TH JANUARY 1920 VOLSTEAD ACT PROHIBITED SALE OF ALCOHOL . . .

LILY LUSH: (in spot) Pretty kids and naughty boys, Lily Lush welcomes you to the Pink Pineapple. Where it's not enough to have a weakness for women you need a great strength. (Artifical laughter). This is the hot spot in town where chunks means diamonds and fur means go as fur as you like! (Laughter). So let the booze flow — live sleazy and speak-eazy. It's a crazy place for crazy people and here is the slob that makes it all happen. Big Diamond Jim Colosimo!
DIAMOND JIM: (He bursts through the truck doors) Thank you. Thank you. Thank you Lily. Keep flowering kid. It's swell to have ya all here on such a special day — my boithday. Yeah, Twenty-five today. That's what clean livin' does for ya. (He looks a dissipated fifty)
   (There is a loud knock and everyone cowers, dives for cover except DIAMOND JIM).
   It's O.K. Relax. Answer the door Lily.
   (CAPONE, GOLDIE and TORRIO enter, sporting carnations and bottles of moonshine)
DIAMOND JIM: Why it's my old friend Johnny Torrio. (He frisks TORRIO). It's great to feel ya John.
TORRIO: It's great to be felt Jim.
   Jim — I want you to meet a new torpedoe on my payroll by the name of AL CAPONE
AL: HI EVERYBODY!

COMPANY: HI AL!
DIAMOND JIM: Al you look in great shape kid. Welcome aboard the booze boat. And tonight kid, you just relax. Enjoy yourself. You have the freedom of the Pineapple.
AL: Thank you Jim. As a matter of fact you might be able to help me. I'm lookin' for a dame.
DIAMOND JIM: (to the COMPANY) He's looking for a dame! We got 'em all sizes kid. What do you fancy? A one dollar whore or an evening of paradise for five 'C's with a free bottle of pineapple joice thrown in.
AL: (smiling) You got me wrong Mr Colosimo. This girl is special and I mean special (He takes BIG JIM's hand and starts to squeeze it). Her name is Mae Coughlin and do not refer to her in any derogatory way cos it kinda distoibs the fireworks inside me! (He has Big Jim in pain)
DIAMOND JIM: (wrenching away injured hand). Hey, you got a real Jumping Jack here John!
TORRIO: Cool it kid!
GOLDIE: Cool it!
TORRIO: (to GOLDIE) Shuddup

> NEWSPANEL ... TORRIO-CAPONE WEEKLY ILLICIT PROFITS $25,000

(The COMPANY AND BIG JIM freeze)
TORRIO: (move downstage right followed by AL and GOLDIE. He speaks aside) I am pleased by this clash of poisonalities — because this speakeasy happens to be one of my filling stations but from these very lucrative proceeds from birds and booze Big Jim has been filling his own tank as well as those of the customers. It is time Big Jim got ready for the long lie down. Tonight is his night. After da cabaret we will give Jim a special boithday present. You understand me Al?
AL: (thumbing in COLOSIMO's direction) Datsa dead?
TORRIO: Datsaright
GOLDIE: Datsa good
COMPANY: Datsa bad
(The FREEZE is broken by BIG JIM's voice)
DIAMOND JIM: Hey! We're all standing around like stooges when we should be swillin' the tipsy-liquor. Pretty soon people will stop frequenting this joint. Al — John pull yourself up a glass of frazzle (He turfs broads out of the table stage right) and watch the high class entertainment we got on tonight. Lily!
Where is that old bag?
Lily. The show. We're waitin' sweetheart.
LILY LUSH: Sure Diamond Jim. Lushes and Lasses we present for your entertainment
(She turns to the two palookas touching her either side) Hey creep — take your hand offa my knee (sweetly to one) not you (with contempt to the other) you!
Ladies and Gents a big hand of fingers for Miss Mae Coughlin, Goldie Kandinski
GOLDIE: Hey that's me!
LILY LUSH: — and the PINK PINEAPPLE PERTIES!
(MAE COUGHLIN and the BOOTLEG BABIES enter — they have loud charleston outfits, boas and feathered or trimmed headbands)

SONG: 'BOOTLEG BABY TRAIN'

MAE & GOLDIE: (very breathy)
THERE'S A SONG THE CATS ARE SINGING
FROM THE EAST SIDE TO THE BRONX
IT'S ALL ABOUT THE BOOTLEG BOOZE
THAT THE BIG BAD BOYS PRODUCE
IT COMES EXPRESS DELIVERY
FROM MIAMI UP TO MAINE
AND WE'RE THE GOILS WHO COLLECT IT
FROM THAT BOOTLEG BABY TRAIN

BABIES: BOOTLEG-BOOTLEG BABIES
BOOTLEG-BOOTLEG BABIES
ANYTHING YOU NEED WE CAN SUPPLY IT
HOW ABOUT A HIGH-BALL?
BOOTLEG BOOTLEG FLOOZIE
BOOTLEG MAKE YOU WOOZIE
DON'T MAKE LOVE ALONE, YOU'LL RUIN YOUR VISION
DOWN WITH PROHIBITION

SO DON'T STAY SINGLE
FIND SOME PALS
START SEEING DOUBLE
WITH BOOZE AND GALS
YES . . TASTE OUR NECTAR, BABY
WE'RE REAL THIRST QUENCHERS, BABY
SO GET ABOARD THE BOOTLEG BABY TRAIN

BOOTLEG BOOTLEG BABIES
BOOTLEG BOOTLEG BABIES
ANYTHING YOU NEED WE CAN PROVIDE IT
HOW ABOUT A SCREW-TOP?
BOOTLEG BOOTLEG HUZZY
BOOTLEG MAKES YOU MUZZY
DRINKING BOOZE WITH US MEANS NAUGHTY NAUGHTIES
SOMEONE TOIN THE LIGHT OUT!

SO MIX A COCKTAIL
DRINK IT DOWN
FORGET TOMORROW
AND PAINT THE TOWN
YOU'LL FIND US CUDDLY, BABY
FILL US WITH BUBBLY BABY
AND GET ABOARD THE BOOTLEG BABY TRAIN

MAE & GOLDIE: THERE'S A BOOTLEG CHOO-CHOO COMING
UP FROM FLO-RA-DEE-DIE-DAY
WITH CRATES AND CRATES OF HIGH CLASS HOOCH
THAT WILL RUIN MOTHER'S DAY
WE SHIP IT OUT OF CUBA
TRUCK IT UP TO PENNSYLVAIN
AND WE'RE THE GOILS WHO COLLECT IT
FROM THAT BOOTLEG BABY TRAIN

BOOTLEG BOOTLEG BABIES
BOOTLEG BOOTLEG BABIES
ANYTHING YOU NEED WE CAN HIGH JACK IT
HOW ABOUT A PUNCTURE
BOOTLEG BOOTLEG LIZZIE
BOOTLEG MAKES YOU DIZZY
LOVIN' US WILL GIVE YOU HEEBIE-JEEBIES
TRY A LITTLE FEELIE!

SO SWIG YOUR LIQUOR
WET YOUR LIPS
GRAB A HOOKER
AND KISS HER QUICK
YES — HELLZA — POPPIN', BABY
OUR CORKZA — POPPIN', BABY
SO CLIMB ABOARD THE BOOTLEG BABY
WE MEAN THAT EXPRESS BABY
CLIMB ABOARD THAT BOOTLEG BABY TRAIN
WOOO-OOOOO!

Dance followed by reprise of middle 8 and last two verses.

EXHIBIT EIGHT: 'BIG JIM'S BOITHDAY PARTY'

(At the end of the song the girls exit giggling and get ready for Party)

MAE: (coming to AL's table) See you when I've changed Al

AL: Sure thing baby

DIAMOND JIM: Hey dat was really somethin'. You know I'm a sucker for a song wid a strong moral message

TORRIO: (leading DIAMOND JIM to one side) Big Jim — a quiet word. You know there is something which gives even greater pleasure than a pretty ditty.

DIAMOND HIM: Yea — what's dat?

TORRIO: Speak him da words, Al

AL: Diamond Jim — BIG JIM. Tonight is your boithday. The boithday of a man who has always strived to keep his bootleg district trouble free.

COMPANY: YEA!

AL: Honest

COMPANY: YEA!

AL: Virginal

GOLDIE: YEA! (They all look at her in disbelief)

AL: As a reward and token of our appreciation for your continued application, Mr Torrio and I have organised for you — Big Jim — a small surprise

DIAMOND JIM: (with disbelief) It's a cake! It's a cake!

TORRIO: Patience Patience (as to a small excited child). Close your eyesies until its time to peekaroojie

DIAMOND JIM: (nearly wetting himself) What is it? What is it?

AL: O.K. You dummies toin down the lights and gimme some boithday type music
(The LIGHTS and BAND oblige)
Datsa Joyous

TORRIO: O.K. Goils bring on da surprise. (They enter with a huge cake 'To Big Jim with love and happy memories) O.K. Take a peeperoo, Big Jim

DIAMOND JIM: (opens one eye at a time) IT IS A CAKE! (nearly in tears) Lily Lily. It's just what I've always wanted
(AL conducts MAE and the GOILS. It is out of tune)
HAPPY BOITHDAY TO YOU
HAPPY BOITHDAY TO YOU
HAPPY BOITHDAY
BIG DIAMOND JIM COLOSIMO (very gabbled)
HAPPY BOITHDAY TO YOU

DIAMOND JIM: Jeez, dat choich music always gets me right dere.
(AL moves up to top right scaffold area where a tommy gun is placed)

LILY LUSH: Here's da knife, boss
TORRIO: Just before you cut the cake, B.J., and we have ourselves a slice of da marzipan fun, it would be stoopid of us not to make use of such an opportoonity
JIM: (To LILY) What's he talkin' about?
LILY: He's talkin' about you
DIAMOND JIM: Yea? Terrific. My favourite subject!
TORRIO: Big Jim as a man of vast experience — I guess dat dere are a few poitenant questions some of the younger members in da rackets would like to ask you. Some poils of wisdom to cast before swine — like young Al here
DIAMOND JIM: Sure thing. Anyway I can help, John. You know da little kids in da street still come runnin' up to me for a nickel sugar-stick. You wanna ask some advice Al?
AL: Sure, Big Jim, I have a simple question for you and I sincerely hope that you can give me da correct answer
DIAMOND JIM: O.K. Fire away!
AL: Dats da answer!

    (The BOITHDAY CAKE opens at the top and the CAKE KILLER produces a sub machine gun. AL has one secreted on the raised area. They blast BIG JIM across the floor and off stage where he is placed in the coffin trolley)
    (THERE IS A MOMENT — SILENCE)

TORRIO: What a tragic accident
GOLDIE: On his boithday too
AL: A sudden and bereaving loss
TORRIO: Al you had better organise things for the funeral. I am too deeply shocked
LILY LUSH: (coming up and slipping her arm in TORRIO'S) Me too — Boss
AL: It is like losing one of da family. Leave the arrangements to me J.T. I will see to it that all is distastefully completed. Punks pick up da garbage (signifying Big Jim's corpse). Goldie ring da florists and order a wreath from O'Banion's shop
GOLDIE: Allright already. Say what would you like written on the card?
AL: (thinking) Er . . 'Suffer da little children to come unto me'
GOLDIE: Jeez. I wish I'd said that. (She exits)
AL: There will now be a few minutes quiet while da Coffin Choristers sing a few verses as a kinda epitaff to accompany Diamond Jim on his journey to the Big Honky Tonk in da sky
    (THE FUNERAL CORTEGE slowly wheel BIG JIM in his coffin centre stage and the COFFIN CHORISTERS stand as a group beside it. Some of the COFFIN BEARERS are still drinking and smoking. There are bottles in the coffin)

SONG: BIG JIM'S CHORALE

    ALACK A DAY BIG JIM IS GONE
    HANG ROSES ROUND HIS ARBOUR
    AND LET US SING HEY NONNY NO
    THEN DUMP HIM IN THE HARBOUR

    SEE DA CLEAR MOON, THE WORLD'S NIGHT EYE
    IS AT OUR WINDOW PEEPING
    SO 'ERE DA SUN DA DEED ESPIES
    LET'S FRISK HIM WHILE HE'S SLEEPING

    THEREFORE AWAKE, MAKE HASTE I PRAY
    UNTO THE PLACE AFFIX-ED
    LAY HIM TO REST, WHERE ANGELS PRAY
    IN CONCRETE READY-MIX-ED

(The CHORISTERS hum quietly below the funeral testimonials)

AL:	Dis was da noblest gangster of dem all
	All de udder mobsters did what dey did
	In envy of great J.T.
	He only in a general honest thought
	And common good to all
	Became a thievin' pigeon
	His life was lousy and the booze
	So mix-ed in him that Nature might
	Stand up and say 'This was a bum'
DIAMOND JIM:	(Suddenly finds a last spark of life) You doity creeps!
	(As he rises in the coffin he is immediately silenced forever with a volley of shots from the CHORISTERS)
	(The coffin is removed)
TORRIO:	According to his virtues, let use him
	Wid all respects and rites of burial
	Within my sedan his bones tonight shall lie
	Most like a hoodlum
	Ordered dishonourably
	So call the party to a close and lets away
	To part da glories of dis happy boithday

EXHIBIT NINE: 'THE RAID'

(The solemnity of the moment is broken by the sudden entrance of RYAN O'HARA and two of his GANGSTERS SQUIRT and GOOFBALL)

RYAN O'HARA: Freeze! Everybody! This is a raid (screams and movement). The party is just about to begin

LILY LUSH: (Bravely stands before him) And what do you intend doin' on this raid? No count O'Hara?

RYAN O'HARA: We're intending a little blood-spillin'

SQUIRT O'HARA: Bootleg lootin'

GOOFBALL: And maybe a little rape!

GOLDIE: (stepping in front of LILY LUSH) Now you look here O'Hara. You can do what you like to the rest of us goils but you just keep your filthy hands offa Lily. O.K.?

LILY LUSH: (Quickly in front of GOLDIE and looking O'HARA straight between the eyes) Shut up Goldie. A raids — a raid!

(The dialogue between the girls and O'HARA is suddenly halted by AL on raised area)

AL: Hit da floor!

(There is the rumble of bullets, chairs fly, fights ensue, screams volley. AL gets his left cheek cut — for convenience a simple streak of lake until the interval when the full scar is made up. At the end of the fight — just the bodies of O'HARA, SQUIRT and GOOFBALL remain — with TORRIO, GOLDIE and AL standing in the silence)

AL: You notice, it's suddenly gone quiet

TORRIO: Kinda peaceful

GOLDIE: Stagnant

AL: (to audience) The reason I have organised this temporary lull in the proceedings is because an important event is about to take place. You see my new girl, Mae, is gonna come in and she's gonna say . . .

MAE: (out front) Hi Al . . . and then he's gonna say

AL: Will you marry me kid?

MAE: And I'm gonna say (she turns to look at him) Yea

TORRIO: Congratulations Al

GOLDIE: We hope you'll both be very happy

TORRIO: Allow me to kiss the new Mrs Capone

GOLDIE: And let me have a nibble outa you tough guy (she kisses him). Hey you cut your face bad
AL: They say a scar gives a guy poisonality
TORRIO: (To AL) Come on youre supposed to kiss the bride (AL and MAE kiss gently)
AL: (softly) Your some potatoe. Are you happy Kid?
MAE: Sure (touching the scar) and you got poisonality
GOLDIE: (snuggling up to TORRIC) Say, why don't you say somethin' nice like that to me?
TORRIO: Shuddup
GOLDIE: Ecstasy
AL: What's it feel like to be a wife — Mrs Capone?
MAE: Kinda funny
GOLDIE: (taking her to one side) Funny? I think you're just plain lucky kid. I wish it could happen to me — all I've ever been is a mistress — you know — the kinda thing that goes between a mister and a matress.
TORRIO: Stop blabbin' Goldie. Go and get the guys to bring the truck round to the side entrance. We'll load this refuse (signifying the bodies) on board, then take a moonlight ride along Harbour Drive and deliver some fresh fish food
    (GOLDIE exits)
MAE: Where are we goin' Al?
AL: Well I thought we might get to bed early or we could . . .
TORRIO: (breaking in) Drive to CHICAGO CITY
MAE: Chicago City? But Mr Torrio Al hasn't even got a car
TORRIO: He has now kid. A hot little Stutz 'bearcat' parked out the back
AL/MAE: Wow!
TORRIO: A small wedding gift to a couple of nice kids
AL/MAE: Thanks a million J.T.
TORRIO: It's nothin' I'm happy to share what little I have. It is now 4 a.m. O.K.? (He holds out fob watch and they look)
AL/MAE: O.K.
TORRIO: Good. You and Mae is going places starting as from now
MAE: What do you mean Mr Torrio?
TORRIO: I mean, kid, that I am sending Al to take over my Chicago interests. You will be my number one. You get 50% of the rake off. You're gonna be rich kids.
AL: I am greatly honoured Mr Torrio
TORRIO: It's O.K.
GOLDIE: (entering) Truck's ready
AL: (turning to the reviving O'HARA'S) Come on. All you stiffs get on your feet and climb aboard the fun wagon. It's time for the cement slippers
    (The O'HARA'S come to, slowly droop off, holding heads and wounds, but GOOFBALL cracks)
GOOFBALL: I don' wanna die I don' wanna die!
AL: Stop over-actin'. There's always a foist time for everythin'
GOLDIE: (taking GOOFBALL'S hand like a child) Yea. Come on. Follow the nice lady.
TORRIO: See you later Big Al — Mae
MAE: Bye Mr Torrio — (he turns, she's forgotten something) . . . Sir! (She grins)

<u>EXHIBIT TEN: 'ON THE ROAD'</u>

MAE: Well Big Al — what are we waitin' for? Let's whistle up that new motor and get ourselves on the road
MAE/AL: To Chicago!
MAE: This is where the story really begins
MAE/AL: Wheeeee!

> NEWSPANEL ... CAPONE TO ORGANISE CHICAGO BOOZE AND VICE ...

(MAE and AL do a circle run down the wings upstage and on the way grab flashy driving clothes as the COMPANY GROUP roll in with cut out cars)

SONG: 'DRIVIN' ALONG ON LOVE'

MAE/AL:
HERE WE GO
YOU AND ME
DRIVIN' ALONG ON LOVE
IT'S THE CRAZY TWENTIES
AND ALL THAT JAZZ
DRIVIN' ALONG ON LOVE
MAE AND BIG AL
DRIVIN' THROUGH THE DAWN
GONNA TAKE CHICAGO BY STORM
BIG AL AND HIS PAL
NOTHIN' BUT THE BEST
RIDIN' THE ROAD TO SUCCESS
YEA.
RIDIN' THE ROAD TO SUCCESS

I LOVE YOU BABY
I LOVE YOU SO MUCH
PUT YOUR ARM AROUND ME
LET'S DOUBLE DE CLUTCH
THOUGH WE'RE OUTA GAS
YOU WON'T HAVE TO SHOVE
COS' THIS KINDA MOTOR
MOTIVATES ON LOVE

(The AL/MAE car is now joined by two other cars left and right upstage)

AL/MAE: PASSENGERS:
HERE WE GO
YOU AND ME
DRIVIN' ALONG ON LOVE
ITS THE CRAZY TWENTIES
AND ALL THAT JAZZ
DRIVIN' ALONG ON LOVE
MAE AND BIG AL
DRIVIN' THROUGH THE DAWN
GONNA TAKE CHICAGO BY STORM
BIG AL AND HIS PAL
NOTHIN' BUT THE BEST
RIDIN' THE ROAD TO SUCCESS
YEA
RIDIN' THE ROAD TO SUCCESS!

(The middle eight and the chorus is reprised and on the last note there is a flash and an explosion. The cars fall to pieces and the COMPANY fall on the floor in a tangled crash freeze) Blackout. Curtain. Car hooters sound as the curtain closes.

> NEWSPANEL ... END OF PART ONE ...

THE SECOND HALF

As the lights come up the Chicago gangs are assembled in groups on the playing area, high and low. CAPONE, MAE, GUSIK (Capone's legal adviser) and ANSELMI and SCALISE (Capone's homicide squad) are standing behind CAPONE who is seated at an office table stage right. GUSIK has a table stage left with legal documents. ALL COMPANY are in suits)

EXHIBIT ELEVEN: 'THE SHARE OUT'

> NEWSPANEL ... CAPONE DIVIDES CHICAGO INTO PROFIT-SHARING GANGDOMS ...

AL: Mr Torrio is very angry
SCALISE: Displeased
ANSELMI: Full of wrath
AL: Wrathful. The reason being that you bums have been knocking off each others livelihoods. Stealing from each other
O'BANION: What's he talkin' about?
ANGELO GENNA: Dat's a lie
JACOB GEISS: I ain't ever stole anything in my life
AL: (slapping the table) Shuddup! Dat is what you punks have been doin'. I am here to see it ceases forthwith
MAE: From now on Chicago is gonna be divided into sections
GANGSTERS: (complain)
AL: Listen! Each section will be the territory of one gang. You set up your own alky cooking centres and sell your bootleg in the clubs of your territory and no other.
HYMIE WEISS: It's not fair
KLONDYKE MILES: I don't like it
GENNA BRUDDER: O'Banion's territory is bigger than any one else's
AL: Close 'em. Ya hear! As has been obsoived by one of Angelo's brudders — some of the aforementioned territories are bigger than what others are
MAE: So we shall share da profits
GANGSTERS: (Uproar)
AL: Hold it. Remember
MAE: United we flourish . . .
AL: Divided we go down da sewer
O'BANION: Hey what are you gettin' outsa dis, Capone?
AL: I don' get nothin' outsa dis, O'Banion. I merely look after your interests. I will see to it that no small time hoodlums break into your parish. Any no-count bum that tries hustling your payroll gets shovelled underground
GUSIK: For which extra service Mr Torrio and Big Al will be taking a small 10% cream off all da Chicago red light and booze takings
HYMIE WEISS: I don' like it
MAE: You don' like it. You don' join. But just remember dat if you don' belong to da organisation ...
ANSELMI: You better start locking your bedroom door at night
SCALISE: Otherwise your wife and kids will be havin' scrambled brains for breakfast
HYMIE WEISS: Upon further consideration. I think it's a very good idea
GENNA BRUDDER: YEA. It's a good idea
O'BANION: I like it
ANGELO GENNA: Sound business proposition
KLONDYKE MILES: I'm joining
JACOB GEISS: Where do I sign?

AL: Hold it Hold it! Foist let us make sure that we have established clearly each territory and its limits. Then I can protect your gang and ensure the smooth running of this beneficial syndicate. Jack Gusik, here, my legal adviser, will be takin' down the names and areas and my two ace gunners ...
SCALISE: John Scalise
AL: ... and ...
ANSELMI: Alberto Anselmi
AL: Will be ensurin' that monthly payments are made on da line wid a smile
ANSELMI: Startin' Monday week
GUSIK: Right gentlemen who is first?
(The individual GANG LEADERS come forward and announce themselves downstage before breaking left and signing GUSIK's document. This to be completed very quickly)
KLONDYKE AND MILES O'DONNELL: Klondyke and ...
MILES: Miles O'Donnell – West side Chicago and Logan Square. (They sign with a big X)
DION O'BANION: Dion O'Banion ...
BUGS MORAN: and Bugs Moran – The Loop district and Circulation Alley (They leave large thumb prints as signatures)
ANGELO GENNA: Angelo Genna. Sicilian Colony, West side on behalf of his four brudders
FIFTH BRUDDER: Five!
ANGELO GENNA: Five Brudders (He signs by sticking a knife into the paper)
HYMIE WEISS: Hymie Weiss – North side and Sauganash (He signs with a little rubber stamp)
SAM SAMOOTS AMATUNA: Sam Samoots Amatuna ...
POLACK JOE SALTIS: And Polack Joe Saltis – Near North side and Lincoln Park (They hand in a printed address card)
JACOB GEISS: Jacob Geiss – The Rialto ... and a few shops my life already (He signs with his jewish spectacles close to the paper in great detail. The other GANGSTERS are intrigued)
BUGS MORAN: Hey what about Spike O'Donnell and the South side?
SAM SAMOOTS AMATUNA: I believe that our colleague and trusted friend Spike O'Donnell is residing at Joliet Penitentiary
GANGSTERS (laugh)
O'BANION: (not laughing) Therefore he is not included in the division of territories
GANGSTERS: Agreed
AL: Thank you gentlemen. We now have real structure
MAE: You no longer require cops and lawyers. You got your own enforcement agency
GUSIK: Mr Capone is very pleased to have your co-operation, gentlemen. He will be available for private consultation here at his new address – the Four Deuces, South Wabash Avenue. You now have the freedom to put into practice any new ventures within your own city limits – but to be frank there is 'no limit' to what can be achieved in Chicago City

  SONG: 'CHICAGO CITY'

CAPONE:	I KNOW WHAT IS GOOD FOR YOU
	IT'S DOWN IN BLACK AND WHITE
MAE &	I AM THE GREAT PROTECTOR
CAPONE:	OF YOUR CASHBOX AND YOUR RIGHTS
MAE & AL:	IF WE CAN TRUST EACH OTHER
SCALISE:	AND ONLY DUPE THE DOPES
ANSELMI:	THEN THIS COULD BE A CITY
GUSIK:	THAT IS FULL OF LOVE AND HOPE
ALL:	CHICAGO
	CHICAGO CITY
	FULL OF SLUGS AND WEALTHY JERKS
	CHICAGO
	CHICAGO CITY

                        IT'S WHERE PERVOITED COPS LURK
                        YOU WANNA RUB YOUR BRUDDER OUT
                        OR FINGER A FINK
                        TOMMY GUN TOMATOES
                        WASH DA BLOOD DOWN DA SINK
                        DRINKS WHERE THERE'S NO LIMIT
                        TO THE DRINKS THAT YOU DRINK
                        TRY CHICAGO
                        CHICAGO
                        CHICAGO CITY
                        ILLINOIS

COMPANY: CHICAGO
            CHICAGO CITY
GOILS: WHERE GOILS ARE TEN CENTS A RIDE
COMPANY: CHICAGO
            CHICAGO CITY
GUYS: WHERE RATS FLOAT IN ON THE TIDE
COMPANY: YOU WANNA GAMBLE ALL YOUR DOUGH
            ON BOOZE AND A LAUGH
            TRY TO BE A BIG SHOT
            AND SCREW DAMES THAT ARE CLASS
            SPEND YOUR LIFE LIKE WATER
            AND END UP ON YOUR ASS
            TRY CHICAGO
            CHICAGO
            CHICAGO CITY
            ILLINOIS

AL & MAE: WE'VE GOT OURSELVES A GOLDMINE
            A GILT EDGED PROPERTY
            AND EACH WILL GET HIS FAIR SHARE
            OF MY GENEROSITY
            JUST TRY NOT TO BE GREEDY
            BE HAPPY WITH YOUR LOT
            COS ANY BUM DISGRUNTLED GETS
            HIS HAT AND HEAD BLOWN OFF!

ALL: CHICAGO
            CHICAGO CITY
            WHERE COPS AND LAWYERS ARE CHEAP
            CHICAGO
            CHICAGO CITY
            WHERE CORPSES LITTER THE BEACH
            YOU WANNA START A RACKET UP
            BE PART OF A CHAIN
            LEARN TO SHOOT A THOMPSON
            THAT WILL TATTOO YOUR NAME
            BANG AS MANY BANG-BANGS
            AS CAN BANG-BANG A GANG
            TRY CHICAGO
            CHICAGO
            CHICAGO CITY
            THAT MEAN OLE WINDY CITY
            CHICAGO

CHICAGO CITY
ILLINOIS
YEAH!

    Reprise last verse with Jimmy Durante voices till 'You wanna start a racket up'
    (When the number ends JOE HOWARD bursts in)
JOE HOWARD: Hey you guys drunk or somethin'. Playing practical jokes. I park my car out front as
    I park it everyday and some joker has bummed it up!
ANSELMI: Whatja talkin' about goof?
HOWARD: Who painted my car bright yellow?
CAPONE: (coming up to him close) I did
JOE HOWARD: (backing off) Dat's O.K. I just wondered if you were gonna give it a second coat?
BUGS MORAN: Who is dis creep
JOE HOWARD: I'm Joe Howard 2300 South Wabash Avenue. Small time hoodlum. I hi-jack booze
    and underprice the big boys. (GANGSTERS growl)
AL: (To GUSIK) Jack read me back the last sentence in the syndicate minutes
GUSIK: I, Al Capone, will see to it dat no 'small time hoodlum' breaks into your parish. Any no-count
    bums that try hustling your payroll will be shovelled underground
JOE HOWARD: Why don't I keep my big mouth shut!
    (AL and GANGSTERS shoot down Howard. He falls into the arms of SCALISE and ANSELMI
    who drag him off past JACOB GEISS)
JACOB GEISS: (a nervous Jew) You shot him. You shot him!
MAE: Don' worry Jacob
AL: We're friends of the family
JACOB GEISS: Oh. That's O.K. I didn't realise you were that close
    (MOOD MUSIC Incidental)
AL: Gentlemen. When shall we all meet again?
    In thunder lightening or in rain?
ANGELO GENNA: When de hurly burly's done
    When the battle's lost and won
O'BANION: Dat will be 'ere da set of sun
BUGS MORAN: Where da place?
KLONDYKE: Upon da heath
MAE: There to meet with?
COMPANY: Big Al! (GANGSTERS exit)
AL: (to MAE) I love ya baby . . . See you boys . . . Nice to see you Angelo, take care of da brudders.
    Don't worry so much Jacob. DION you keep da peace now — O.K.?
O'BANION: You can trust me. (He laughs at audience)
MAE: Bye boys. See ya around

EXHIBIT TWELVE: 'NUMERO ONE'

    (All GANGSTERS exit except for AL, MAE, GUSIK and the returned SCALISE and
    ANSELMI)
AL: (To Anselmi and Scalise) Cover the doors (They do so). Jack get those agreements duplicated.
    (GUSIK picks them up). Well Mae. What do you think of your new home? The Four Deuces?
MAE: D'ere ain't nothin' here
AL: Dat's on account of I want you to choose somethin' to put in here
MAE: (looking around) Well — it's big, run-down and the paints peelin' but with a little fixing it has
    real possibilities
GOLDIE: (head appearing round SCALISE) Some one talkin' about me?
AL: It's O.K. let it in
MAE: (looking at bedraggled and wrecked GOLDIE) Goldie. Watcha doin' here? I thought you were on
    vacation with Mr Torrio

GOLDIE: You ain't hoid then?
AL: (getting three glasses of booze from R table) Hoid what?
GOLDIE: Mr Torrio got guzzled on Clyde Avenue
MAE: You poor kid
GOLDIE: There's bits of him left in Jackson Park Hospital, but only me — and Mrs Torrio was allowed to see him
AL: Who did it, this deed?
GOLDIE: They're sayin' that it was O'Banion's boys. He arranged the bump off to happen while he was at your big meetin',
AL: Dat doity bum
MAE: Are you allright Goldie?
GOLDIE: Sure. I only came over cos I'm kinda unemployed now and I wondered if you could use me Al?
AL: What ain't been used yet, I shall use. You're on the pay-roll
GOLDIE: Sweet talker
MAE: You gonna let O'Bannion get away with that killing Al?
AL: I shall deal with that piece of business when the time is right . . . I've had my eyes on those two big shots O'Banion and Moran. Meanwhilst they need a little scarin'. Alberto!
ANSELMI: Boss? (he sprints to his side)
AL: Deliver in gift-wrapped paper a couple of 'do-it-yourself' embalming kits to those two fat hats
ANSELMI: I like it. I like it
AL: John
SCALISE: Mr Capone (sprints to other side)
AL: Tomorrow you will quietly collect the small tattered remains of our beloved and late lamented Mr Torrio from the morgue slab and arrange to have him placed in a . . (He looks to GOLDIE for a decision)
GOLDIE: (Over sugary music) Bronze casket . .
AL: With a silk lining of . . ?
GOLDIE: Forget-me-not-blue
AL: You got taste Goldie. I like dat
MAE: And a heart-shaped wreath from both of us signed 'Mae and Al — Your pals'
AL: Poetry kid. Pure poetry. O.K. Move
ANSELMI/SCALISE: Sure thing boss. Right away
AL: Now J.T. has demised. You know what this means don't you?
GOLDIE: YEA. It means you are Numero One
MAE: 'The' Man
AL: Exactly thus. So as I am now in big business, I shall need more elbow room, more muscle for development
GOLDIE: Try weightlifting
AL: Shuddup
GOLDIE: Hey. It's just like the old days
MAE: Goldie. This is important!
AL: (Music) To expand my empire — I need new territories, new districts — so that the people can render unto Capone da things dat are Capone's. In return I will serve da nation by providing prompt delivery of booze to all speakeasies — so that a man may drink and misabuse a dame in peace
GOLDIE: I didn't understand any of that — but it sure as hell sounds good
MAE: Al. If you need to expand into new districts you could do what Mr Torrio used to do. Collect all da facts and figures about every territory and then take over da richest
AL: Assess the incomings and outcomings of prosperity?
MAE: Dat's right
GOLDIE: J.T. used this big 'ticker-tape' type thing. He used to feed in all his . . er constructive ideas and then the big machine used to tell him which places made the most profit
AL: I am excited by this idea of mine — I shall commence negotiations to purchase such a monster
GOLDIE: Why bother. J.T.'s machine is still here
MAE: Well bring it on Goldie. Bring it on

AL: Yea. Produce the clockwork
   (A Tower is wheeled on. There are nobs and dials which can alter its pitch, volume and speed. The tower is covered by the TICKER-TAPE KIDS who sing and dance the piece on the tower with mechanical movements — like a large clockwork toy)
AL: I am deeply impressed. How does it work?
GOLDIE: Mr Torrio just fed his figures in here and the answer used to come out up there (She points to Newspanel)
MAE: O.K. You feed in the details and I'll pull the handle
AL: (Addressing the Newspanel) Ticker-Tape Ticker-Tape on the wall,
   Which is da fairest district of dem all?
   (MAE pulls handle and the machine works)

SONG: 'THAT OLD SLICK TICKER-TAPE RAG'

   WHEN YOU FEED THE FIGURES IN
   AND YOU PUSH THE DATA THROUGH
   THE DIGITS GO SCOOBEDOO
   THERE'S A KINDA CLANK
   IN OUR TELEGRAPH BANK
   AND THE CIRCUITS TRY TO LOOP DA LOOP
   THERE'S A WICKED TYPE OF REFLEX
   IN THE AUTOMATIC INDEX
   AND THE STORE LOCATORS ARE FULL
   THERE'S A KINDA HONK
   IN OUR CLANG-CLANG-CLANG
   GOT A SSSS-SSSS-SSSSS IN THE SPOOL
   BUT DON'T GET FRENETIC
   COS IT'S SIMPLY MAGNETIC
   AND THE ANSWER IS ON ITS WAY
   MMM MATHEMATICAL
   QUITE FANTASTICAL
   THAT OLD SLICK TICKER-TAPE RAG

AL: I shall now vary the input by means of altering these dials. This way I will ascertain fuller information

AL turns up HIGH PITCH:	WHEN YOU FEED THE FIGURES IN AND YOU PUSH THE DATA THROUGH THE DIGITS GO SCOOBEDOO
AL turns LOW PITCH:	THERE'S A KINDA CLANK IN OUR TELEGRAPH BANK AND THE CIRCUITS TRY TO LOOP DA LOOP
AL turns VOLUME UP:	THERE'S A WICKED TYPE OF REFLEX IN THE AUTOMATIC INDEX AND THE STORE LOCATORS ARE FULL
VOLUME DOWN:	THERE'S A KINDA 'HONK' IN OUR CLANG CLANG CLANG GOT A SSS-SSS-SSS IN THE SPOOL

Speed dial goes to DANGER! Song and chorus get faster and faster until loses control	BUT DON'T GET FRENETIC COS IT'S SIMPLY MAGNETIC AND THE ANSWER IS ON ITS WAY MMM MATHEMATICAL QUITE FANTASTICAL THAT OLD SLICK TICKER TAPE I MEAN TICKER TAPE (BANG!!)

(The machine collapses and all the COMPANY collapse on the tower — there is a moment and then they look up)

>THAT OLD SLICK TICKER TAPE RAG!
>OOO!

MAE: Here comes the message Al

> NEWSPANEL APRIL 1924... 'TAKE CICERO'...

(During the Newspanel the Tower is struck)

AL: Take Cicero! That's it. Why didn't I think of that before?

MAE: Jeez, Cicero. That's the wealthiest suburb in Cook County

GOLDIE: There's a lotta rich bums live d'ere too

AL: Mae. I want you outa town during the Cicero elections. I shall take that place lock, stock and mayor and it's bound to get hot. So you take a vacation

MAE: Sure Al. And I'll take Momma Capone with me O.K.?

AL: O.K. Scalise — Anselmi. Fetch Momma Capone

SCALISE/ANSELMI: Sure boss

AL: (calling) Gusik! You get this place fixed up I want telephones, manicure, barber and spaghetti sandwiches. Now!

GUSIK: Immediately Mr Capone

GOLDIE: Hey. What shall I do?

AL: You (Al beckons her towards him then sticks his finger on her nose) You get yourself a face-lift, some decent clothes and from this day on... Goldie... You get to light my cigars... day and ... night.

GOLDIE: Oooo! Nocturnal ignition. That's my kinda candy. (She engulfs AL and spots MAE looking disapprovingly)

MAE: Take your clams off him, Goldie

AL: (turning on Mae) Whatja talking about? Business is business. Don't come the old ironsides with me. Just get my Momma outa here and somewhere safe — and take care of her — these days she's nervous and old. (She enters in a wheelchair being pushed by SCALISE) Not THAT OLD!

MOMMA CAPONE: (very quiet) I'm sorry Al, the legs a notta so gooda as they used to be — (very loud) and all the time people is shoutin' — it's gotta so I can't get a word in upwards

MAE: Who's shoutin' at you Momma? (AL sits
    (AL sits and five of the COMPANY shave him)

MOMMA CAPONE: (signifying SCALISE) He is

SCALISE: I'm sorry Mr Capone. It's just that yesterday she starts screaming she wants to go to the opera and I wanted to go to the theatre (smugly). But in the end we came to an agreement

AL: What was the opera like?

SCALISE: It was O.K.

MAE: Momma. You are coming with me for a little holiday. Allright?

MOMMA CAPONE: In da sun?

MAE: In da sun

MOMMA CAPONE: Like Italy?

MAE: Like Italy

MOMMA CAPONE: Good. Old Italian women need lotsa sun
AL: Now Momma is d'ere anything you would like before you leave?
MOMMA CAPONE: Si. What I would really like is one of those bigga drinks in a long glass — full of nuts, cream, chianti and cherries. I don't a know what a you call it but I can describe it.
MAE: (laughing) Momma — you just described Florida. Dat's where we are going for our holiday
AL: Si Momma. You go to Florida. Have a lotsa fun. And lotsa big drinks eh? (He kisses her or if shaving blows her a kiss)
MOMMA CAPONE: You're a gooda boy Alphonso. Your father (She smiles but on reflection it turns to a sneer) be plenty proud of his boy. Never did we think you would grow up to be important politician
GOLDIE: (out front) Life's full of surprises like that
AL: You help Mae get the things packed and watch your mouth. (He wipes soap off face and throw towel at barber. They exit)
GOLDIE: Okay. (She exits)
MAE: See you in a few days Al. Take care
AL: Say kid, if you see any nice real estate down that way, den feel free to poichase a small summer retreat
MAE: You betcha (blows him a kiss)
SCALISE: (To Momma) This way Mrs Capone (he wheels her off)
MOMMA CAPONE: (To SCALISE) All right you don'ta have to shout all da time — you wanna the people to think we not a happy family. (ALL on stage turn and grin at audience for a frozen second)
AL: O.K. Gusik. You got your book? (secretive)
GUSIK: Certainly sir
AL: Right. Add to the other list a new wardrobe of suits — some flash and snappy, some for evenings and some for funerals
GUSIK: (writing carefully, he is a careful man) F.u.n.e.r.a.l.s.
AL: As soon as Mrs Capone and my wife have departed, book the blue suite at the Hawthorne Hotel and fill it with classy dames and good whisky.
GUSIK: (Writing) W.h.i.s.k.y.
AL: Now tell that Goldie dame to come and light my cigar. (GUSIK exits)
AL: (Soliloquising to audience over INCIDENTAL MUSIC)
    Now you people of Cicero
    Take pity of your town and of your people
    Whiles yet my soldiers are in my command
    (At this point ANSELMI, SCALISE and GOLDIE enter carrying the military campaign table. They freeze on the word 'command')
AL: Whiles yet the cool and temperate winds of grace
    O'er blows the filthy and contagious clouds
    Of heady moider, spoil and villainy
AL: To woik! Scalise. How many guys have I in my personal bodyguard?
SCALISE: Countin' us two?
AL: Countin' you two
SCALISE: Seven hundred
AL: Think of dat. That guy Jesus only had twelve palookas woikin' for him and I got seven hundred. Dat's gotta be good news. (He takes out cigar with flourish but there is no reaction from GOLDIE)
ANSELMI: Hey screwball. The King's cigar (whispered)
GOLDIE: Ooops sorry (She lights it)
AL: Now we gotta lot of organisin' to do to ensure we conquer Cicero in da election. The pollin' booths open in a few minutes — we gotta make sure that the citizens are aware of da new candidate and vote for him.
    ANSELMI! the map of operations (ANSELMI unrolls military map on table)
    Pointer! (SCALISE hands him a wooden map-pointer)
    Coat! (ANSELMI places astrakhan coat over his shoulders like a German Officer)
    Glasses! (GOLDIE flicks on the lighter)

GLASSES! (Goldie takes dark glasses from bag and puts them on herself, AL snatches them off her and puts them on)
    (The business is interrupted by a TELEPHONE ringing on TABLE S.R. as spot comes up on KONVALINKA in telephone booth cut out on raised platform stage L). The whole group ss run across to the right table and AL picks up the phone)
AL: Ed Konvalinka?
KONVALINKA: Yea
AL: Everythin' fixed?
KONVALINKA: Sure we put good boys in for all the council positions. Jo Klenha for Mayor and close friends of the family as town clerk and town attorney
AL: Good!
    (Spot comes up on booth stage R containing LOMBARDO, the phone on the table S.L. rings The group dash across the stage to the new phone)
AL: (hearing gun fire)
LOMBARDO: Al? This is Tony Lombardo
AL: It sounds heavy down there
LOMBARDO: Si. Just a little fireworks
AL: Tony. I want muscle and artillery on every corner of the street mit gangsters cars patrolling ze outzide of de polling booths. Thompsons and .45's at A, B and C blocks
    (SCALISE and ANSELMI move toy cars and tanks into positions on the map)
LOMBARDO: Every citizen will be persuaded to put his cross against the right name
    (The spot on LOMBARDO blacks out and comes up centre playing area on GUSIK. The GROUP run to the centre table)
GUSIK: I fixed up for you to have some publicity shots with Mr Jack Sharkey the World Champ directly after tonight's victory
AL: Datsa good I must have a propaganda
    (Spot blacks out on centre area. PHONE rings table left which ANSELMI answers)
ANSELMI: Hello? Yea. Hey, d'ere's a guy here askin' if you can give a donation to the Cicero Kids Orphanage. What shall I do?
AL: Send him two orphans! (He holds out cigar for GOLDIE to relight. She does so)
    (PHONE rings at centre table. Spot comes up on centre playing area on MAE)
AL: Hello?
MAE: Al this is Mae
AL: You O.K. sweetheart?
MAE: Sure. Say Al do you like kids?
AL: Sure I went to school with 'em
MAE: Only the doc says to expect a kid after Christmas
AL: Hey that's terrific — I'm gonna have a baby! It's gonna be a boy. Just like his Poppa and he'll climb upon my knee . . .
GOLDIE: (like Jolson) Sonny Boy
AL: Shuddup. On foither consideration I *like* dat. We *shall* call him Sonny. I decided
    (The PHONE rings at table left. Spot picks up LOMBARDO under tin helmet)
LOMBARDO: Al. The County Judge has sworn in another seventy cops for re-inforcements!
AL: Don't give me excuses. Advance at all costs. Send in more tanks mit bigger bombs!
    (PHONE rings at centre table. AL rushes to it in state of panic)
AL: Hello! (Looks at GOLDIE with pained expression) It's for you. Your parents
GOLDIE: Hello Momma. It's crazy to hear your voice again! How are ya? Oh I'm sorry Poppa. Is Momma there? Hello Mom? It's me . . . Goldie . . . Goldie. Goldie Kandinski — your daughter remember? Yea dat's right — the pretty one (SCALISE, ANSELMI and AL turn away in disgust) How's your back Mom? You ain't been woikin' lately? Now Mom about that recipe for blueberry . . .
    (PHONE rings table right)
AL: Hold it! It's the election result comin' through. Anselmi take down every word

GUSIK (in centre spot) We did it Al. Cicero is now part of t'ie Capone Empire. We move the booze trucks in tomorrow and start decoratin'
    INCIDENTAL MUSIC
ANSELMI: The day is yours
SCALISE: Long live the king
AL: (taking ANSELMI's record of the words) This is an historical document — to be preserved among the sacred archives of gangland. I have looked upon the face of Cicero! What is dat skyscraper dat stands hard by?
GOLDIE: Dey call it da Cicero Tower
AL: Den call we dis the field of Cicero. Fought on the day of April Fool Nineteen hundred and twenty-four (He holds out the sacred document which GOLDIE instinctively sets fire to with the lighter — as they extinguish the flames the newspanel flashes)

> NEWSPANEL ... CICERO PROFITS $100,000 A WEEK ...

BLACKOUT

LIGHTS UP

EXHIBIT FOURTEEN: 'THE DEATH OF O'BANION'

    (Al steps to talk to the audience as principals exit and the set is prepared on the darkened stage for the MIAMI sequence. AL is in a spotlight)
AL: It is time we had a serious blab, while they get ready for a little celebration I am havin' in Miami. Lotsa goils, lotsa laffs. My kinda lifestyle. I need da rest. But before I relax in da sun there is one small job still to be attended to. I thought you would poisonally be interested in how we take sweet revenge on bums dat keep steppin' outa line. Hey you creeps give me some medical music will ya (INCIDENTAL MUSIC). Those of a noivous disposition should hide under da chairs. (He shouts off) DION O'BANION! I wanna talk to you

> NEWSPANEL ... CAPONE ORDERS DEATH OF DION O'BANION ...

O'BANION: (entering slowly from wings) Is dis da time?
AL: Datsaright. You scared of dyin'
    (SCALISE and ANSELMI comb his hair, straighten his tie; pamper him before putting a white coat on him back to front like a straight jacket)
O'BANION: No. It's just come at an inconvenient time
    (As AL speaks GUSIK brings in gun and white gloves on a silver tray which AL proceeds to put on. It is all quiet and surgical)
AL: I heard dat when you guzzled Johnny Torrio you thought you would be the guy at da top of da pile. It ain't quite woiked out dat way, huh?
O'BANION: No. When I got down to it I found I wasn't up to it
AL: (gloves on) Dat is true (O'BANION is turned round back to audience. ANSELMI squeezes blood on face or temple, SCALISE places cloth bag over his head)
AL: Dat is true ... slug. But now you are gonna get down even foither. Meet my personal gravediggers (SCALISE and ANSELMI now have baseball bats in their hands)
    (AL walks up close and whispers into the bag) Goodbye O'Banion. (O'BANION is clubbed four times in slow motion, the group saying the word 'Boff'. He finishes on his knees as AL steps forward with the gun they all shout BANG! as he fires it into his temple. The cloth is removed to display death and blood. AL walks up and closes O'BANION's eyes and says)
AL: Sweet Dreams O'Banion. (He walks a little stage right then turns to say) Get it outa here!
    (O'BANION is dragged off)
    The LIGHTS fade and in the darkness the COOCHEE CRUISERS come into position while newspanel flickers)

> NEWSPANEL ... 5 APRIL 1927 THOMPSON ELECTED MAYOR OF 'CROOK COUNTY ...

EXHIBIT FIFTEEN: MIAMI

(The lights come up very bright and sunny there are fleecy clouds scudding across the cyclorama. The girls are all in swimsuits the boys in white flannels, pullovers, white shirts and cravats. There is a silly gaiety as on Scott and Zelda's yacht. On the scaffold there are lifebelts and signs marked the S.S. KITCHY KOO!)

SONG: 'SAILIN' ON THE SOOPER SALTY SEA'

COMPANY: (A round)
    CRUSING TO THE SUNSHINE STATE
    ON THE 'ITCHY KITCHY KOO'
    SAILIN' TO MIAMI BEACH
    ON THIS DREAM BOAT MADE FOR TWO

> NEWSPANEL ... 1928 CAPONE BUYS PALM ISLAND VILLA, MIAMI ...

    OH BABY IT'S COOCHEE TIME   (They dance on main and raised
    KISSIN' CUDDLIN' ON THE BRINE areas — a Charleston)
    WHILE SILVER AEROPLANES WRITE
    'I LOVE YOU' IN THE CLEAR BLUE SKY
    O ITCHY KITCHY KOO
    BOO BEE DOO BEE DOO BEE DOO
    SAILIN' ON THE SOOPER SALTY SEA.EE
    SAILIN' ON THE SOOPER SALTY SEA
    BOO BOO BEE DOO!

    OH BABY WE AIN'T REFINED
    LIKE THE VANDERBILTS SO DIVINE
    WE DRINK AT JACK DELANEY'S
    AND WE DINE ON WEST FORTY-NINE
    OH ITCHY KITCHY KOO
    BOO BEE DOO BEE DOO BEE DOO
    SAILIN' ON THE SOOPER SALTY SEA-EE
    SAILIN' ON THE SOOPER SALTY SEA
    BOO BOO BEE DOO!

(At the end of the number they all jolt forward as if docking. MAE enters from the wing as white Spanish garden furniture and palm tree are set. She wears a stylish cream summer dress)

GIRL 1: Hey. We're here
GIRL 2: Miami, Florida!
GIRL 3: Lead me to Palm Beach
GIRL 4: Hiya Mae. (They crowd round her)
MAE: Hi. Welcome to the new home
GIRL 5: Congratulations with the baby boy
GIRL 6: Watja call him?
MAE: Sonny Boy
GIRL 5: Climb upon my knee, Son. . .
MAE: Someone's done that already
GIRL 2: Goofball
GIRL 5: Soorryy

MAE: (upset) I didn't realise that Al was bringing guests. I kinda thought that he was just gonna come on his own to see the kid ... and all

GIRL 5: No! He said it was gonna be a big party like the orgy we had at the Hawthorne Hotel after the Cicero elec· (she has goofed)

MAE: Hawthorne Hotel? What are you talkin' about?

GIRL 3: Why can't you keep your big mouth shut!

GIRL 4: Look Mae, would you rather we just left?

MAE: (brightening) No dat's O.K. It'll be kinda nice havin' company. I miss Chicago.

GIRLS: That's great Mae. Thanks a million. Look at that beach (The girls squeal and giggle until Mae calls their attention)

MAE: Look ... there's blue water in the pool, boats to play with in the harbour, food in the Spanish garden and lotsa booze everywhere — most of it is Momma Capone's!

(As the girls are laughing we hear the voice of Momma Capone offstage. She is shouting. She is wearing dark glasses. She is wheeled on in a vivid bath wrap and being massaged on a trolley by RUDY THE MASSEUR — he is camp)

MOMMA CAPONE: Whatsa all da shoutin' about. It's so I can't makea myself be felt. Isn't that right Rudy?

RUDY: You never tell a lie, Mrs Capone

MAE: I'm sorry Momma, but Al has called a convention, a business meeting — it's just politics

MOMMA CAPONE: Politickets. Politickets. I hate Politickets. That's all I hear in dis house. Isn't that right Rudy?

RUDY: You've never told a lie yet, Mrs Capone

MOMMA CAPONE: I'm sicka down to here (Rudy slaps her bum) wid politickets. (To the audience) Why doesn't he shoota dem all and get on with it?

MAE: He tries Momma. He really tries. You tell her Rudy

RUDY: Hear no evil — speak no evil

MOMMA CAPONE: Hey — you pressing too hard. You wanna bruise Momma Capone?

MAE: Momma, there's gonna be a lotta people here, so let Rudy finish you off on the lawn and have another big drink, eh?

MOMMA CAPONE: Ha. They wanta get rid of me. Allrighta. (She turns it on and it affects the company). I'm an olda woman. Nobody don'ta want me no more. Not even my big shot son, Alphonso. Never mind I still gotta my Rudy to look after me eh?

RUDY: Time for walkies gorgeous

(As RUDY pushes her off on the trolley MOMMA pinches a drink from one of the COOCHEE GIRLS, she swigs it and immediately starts off)

MOMMA CAPONE: Hey! Whata you people doin' all over da carpet. Get outa here!

(Immediately on the opposite side of the stage AL accompanied by an entourage of GOLDIE, SCALISE, ANSELMI and GUSIK enter. AL is wearing a bright bathing robe over his suit but still wears a fedora and a big cigar. The GANGSTERS and GOLDIE are self consciously holding beach balls and buckets and spades and wear Captain Webb swimsuits)

AL: Hey! Anybody at home?

MAE: Al! It's great to see you. You're lookin' great

AL: I feel great

(The BOYS on the KITCHY KOO walk around with drinks and food on trays)

AL: Howsa my boy?

MAE: He's fine. Keeps askin' after his Poppa

AL: (Suddenly ignores her when he sees the girls) Hiya Girls!

GIRLS: Hiya Al!

(The GIRLS run past MAE ostracising her unwittingly as they cluster round AL who sits in one of the white garden chairs)

GIRL 1: Is it true that you rubbed out Spike O'Donnell?

GIRL 2: Dion O'Banion?

GIRL 3: Hymie Weiss?

GIRL 4: Joe Esposito?
GOLDIE: Bugs Moran?
    (There is a moment)
AL: We ain't got round to that guy yet — nobody told you to write the next chapter. Dumbelle!
    (He pulls out a cigar. GOLDIE pulls out a banana to light it with. He knocks it away and she lights it correctly)
MAE: (quietly) Al?
AL: (full of himself) You shoulda been at O'Banion's funeral. Beautiful. Gusik you tell 'em — you do these poetic kinda bits betta than me
    INCIDENTAL MUSIC
GUSIK: There was twenty pallbearers in tuxedos — a silk American flag topped with a brass eagle
ANSELMI: Seventeen carloads of flowers and an Irish silk flag
SCALISE: Silver angels stood at his head and feet, d'ere heads bowed (He repeats it and they all bow heads) Bowed! (One girl suffering says 'Jeez')
GUSIK: Ten candles burned in solid gold candlesticks. Beneath da casket — a marble slab that supported his inscription
SCALISE: And the choir sang 'Nearer my God to Thee'
AL: (Stands. He and they are all near to tears) And - And - And you know what - it only - it only cost me ten thousand dollars. (He cracks) Say get me a drink willya. I'm cracking up here (waiter comes with drink) a bigger one you creep! (He immediately turns without stopping and exits)
MAE: (louder) Al? (AL ignores her)
GOLDIE: I sure hated that O'Banion guy
ALL: Yea
GOLDIE: And I sure hate that Bugs Moran. Yuk!
AL: Hey Scalise you got some news on dose Moran boys. Is dat right?
SCALISE: Oh yea -er - I accidentally ran over three of the Moran bums on Forty Fourth Street, yesterday.
AL: What did you do wid 'em?
SCALISE: I buried 'em in concrete
AL: Are you sure dey was dead?
SCALISE: Well, two of 'em said dat dey wasn't — but you know what liars those Moran boys are.
    (ALL laugh)
MAE: (suddenly and unexpectedly the mirth is broken) AL!
AL: (there is a silence) Yea . . . What?
MAE: I keep talkin' to you and you don' listen none
AL: (irritated) I'm dealing with business. I don't have to answer to you for nuddin'
MAE: No? What about all these floozies you brought down here with ya? (The GIRLS back off apprehensively). The Hawthorne Hotel party? And how come Goldie lights your cigar in such a familiar way!
AL: What are you talkin' about. What ARE you talkin' about? Hey? How I live and woik in Chicago is my business. I make a lotta money for you. Classy clothes. Classy houses. So get offa my back and shut up
GOLDIE: Al don't shout — you'll get ulcers
AL: (whirls on her) I don't get ulcers. I give 'em!
MOMMA CAPONE: (appears on trolley) Whatsa all the shoutin' about!
AL: Get her outa here! (She is whisked back as fast as she entered) Gusik!
GUSIK: Mr Capone?
AL: Pack everything up. We're going back to Chicago, My day has been spoiled
GUSIK: Now?
AL: Now!
GUSIK: Certainly Mr Capone
MAE: (Coming down to him) I'm sorry Al — it's just . . .

AL: Just nothin' O.K. (turns to COMPANY) All of you creeps get outa here. You're all leeches. You all live offa me. Put back the food and booze and clear out. Goldie — you're drivin' back wid me. Scalise and Anselmi you follow in the armoured car behind. And Goldie . . .

GOLDIE: Boss?

AL: (he looks at MAE) I want lotsa goils and one special laid on for me tonight. It's gonna be colder than I thought

MAE: Al please don't leave like this. Sonny wants to see you. And the little me that's me . . . needs ya . . . bad

AL: Dis is da way I'm gonna leave because dis is da way I live. Remember — nobody tells me what to do. I am the TOP MAN. Not even people . . . I love . . . tell me what to do. (He starts to take off wrap) Oh yea — tomorrow is Valentine's Day. Read the newspapers. I'll arrange a special suprise for ya . . . sweetheart. (He throws wrap on floor and storms out)

MAE: (running after him) Al . . . Al (She picks up wrap and places it on the chair, she touches it intimately) (To audience) I've known lotsa guys. Loved some of them. You weep a lotta tears that way. But never till now have I ever loved one who makes me hope that one day — just one day — that he'll care and maybe if I'm lucky need me (She sits on a stool stage L in a tight spot)

SONG: 'NEVER 'TIL NOW'

MAE: WHEN HE LIES BESIDE ME IN THE DARK CHICAGO NIGHT
I LEAN ON MY ELBOW AND TRACE MY FINGER ON HIS FACE
KISS COOL LIPS ONTO HIS SKIN
BREATHE LOVE INTO HIS SHOULDERS
HOPING HE'LL WAKE TO ME
PRAYING HE'LL REACH FOR ME
LYING ALONE AND LOST IN THE SHEETS
BUT WHAT DO YOU DO WITH A MAN
THAT JUST WANTS TO ACQUIRE
WHO DOESN'T KNOW THE DIFFERENCE BETWEEN LOVE AND DESIRE
THAT'S WHY HE HURTS ME BAD
AND THE LITTLE ME THAT'S ME
SAYS NEVER 'TIL NOW
NO NEVER 'TIL NOW
HAVE I LOVED ONE
LOVED JUST ONE
WHO MAKES ME HAPPY IN THE HOPE
THAT HE'LL CARE.

WHY DOES HE TRY TO BUY MY LOVE
WITH FURS AND PEARLS AND FANCY JUNK
IS HE BLIND HE CANNOT SEE
THAT MY LOVE FOR HIM IS FREE
THAT I CAN ONLY LIVE IN HIM
FIND MYSELF WHEN I'M WITH HIM
THAT I AM ONLY HALF A WOMAN
'TIL I HOLD HIM IN THE CIRCLE OF MY LOVE.

WHEN HE SLIPS AWAY FROM ME IN THE EARLY MORNING MIST
I WAKE COLD WITH A START AND WIPE TEARS FROM MY WINDOWPANE
TO FIND STREETS SO EMPTY AND BARE
THAT I'M FRIGHTENED AND FEEL SCARED
KNOWING HE'S GONE FROM ME
FEELING THE HURT IN ME
SWIMMING TO MY EYES SO I CAN'T SEE
SO WHAT DO YOU DO WITH A MAN

	THAT JUST WANTS TO CLIMB HIGHER
	WHO LIKE THE CIGARETTE YOU SHARED, STUBS YOU OUT IN THE FIRE
	THAT'S WHY HE HURTS ME BAD
Spot	AND THE LITTLE ME, THAT'S ME
starts to	SAYS NEVER 'TIL NOW
tighten	NO NEVER 'TIL NOW
on head	HAVE I LOVED ONE
and	LOVED JUST ONE
shoulders	WHO MAKES ME HAPPY IN THE HOPE
only	THAT ONE DAY
	HE'LL CARE.

<u>EXHIBIT SIXTEEN: 'THE VALENTINE'S DAY MASSACRE'</u>

As the lights fade on MAE, we hear the sound of a clock ticking loudly 'tick-tock' 'tick-tock' this ominous sound is continuous. The lights come up on the central playing area. Very dimly we see three figures in a freeze, there are boxes of Bathouse Gin stacked stage right. As the clock fades we hear the first phrase of RHADAMES ARIA from AIDA sung by an Italian opera singer. He is dressed in opera cloak, white gloves and tails. He is like the 'phantom of the opera' and as he stands on the raised area stage right AL stands in the centre raised area watching the proceedings. He has paid the singer to serenade the slaughter. This aria was AL CAPONE'S favourite piece of opera. After the first phrase the figures change positions and then in a slow balletic manner four more gangsters enter, they shake hands, but their movements are suspicious, they are furtive. One of the group calls the others round and a DUMB SHOW takes place. He points to an imaginary letter and shows them the details. They cluster around and nod in affirmation. He points to the stacks of boxes, they again nod then split all over the stage and check their personal guns (in mime). Bullets and chambers O.K. Return guns and then form a chain as they pass the stacks from stage right to stage left and off. As they are passing the booze, one of the gangsters opens a box and takes out a bottle of booze and pulls out cork with his/her teeth — the bottle is passed along the line and they sample the brew. At that moment two men disguised as cops enter stage right and left downstage they have 500 watt lamps attached to trolleys which they point straight at the audience, they searchlight them around the auditorium. Four KILLERS enter and the gangsters freeze. They line up facing the audience, then on a signal all hell let's loose and the KILLERS machine-gun the audience. Then as quickly the lights swivel round onto the GANGSTERS just two bars before the aria ends they machine gun the GANGSTERS who hit the walls, scaffolding and are absolutely still as we hear the last note of the aria in the silence.

A spotlight comes up on a radio on the raised area stage left and we hear this announcement:

<u>RADIO</u>: This is the National Broadcasting Company. Chicago City was today stunned by a brutal massacre perpetrated at the S.M.C. Cartage Company Garage. It is the most staggeringly violent of the gangland killings.

NEWSPANEL ... CHICAGO SPEAKEASIES TOTAL 20,000 ... WEEKLY TAKE $6,260,000 ...
500 GANGSTERS SLAIN FROM 1923-26 ...

The henchmen of Bugs Moran walked into a gruesome trap. Thinking it was a routine police search they allowed themselves to be mutilated by gunfire. All seven men have died. Capone is suspected of the crime but so far there is no concrete evidence. This is Hamilton Bridges of Station WJZ signing off — meanwhile here is a brand new tune from the horn of Louis Armstrong playing at The Savoy Ballroom . . . (music fades out . . .)

<u>AL</u>: (shouts) Toin off da radio!

There is a BLACKOUT (during which the KILLERS and GANGSTERS vacate the area. As the lights come up the OPERA SINGER comes towards AL. He is to be paid off for duties rendered)

AL: Maestro, Grazie. I enjoyed that (He hands him a thick envelope full of money)
SINGER: Prego. A pity about the mess. They seemed nicea young people
AL: Si (The SINGER exits)
AL: Hey Shoe shine!
    (A SHOE SHINE BOY enters with his box and brushes — AL lifts his shoe onto the box and the boy works very hard indeed)
AL: You do these shoes well kid. You get yourself a 10 dollar bill. O.K.?
SHOE-SHINE: Sure Mr Capone (He works even harder)
AL: You know somethin' kid? I envy you
SHOE-SHINE: Me — Mr Capone?
AL: (mimicking the boy) Me — Mr Capone? Yea you . . . What's your name boy?
SHOE-SHINE: Gino sir
AL: Well Gino. Once I used to do jobs like this. Yea. I even washed dishes in a restaurant until I met Johnny Torrio and Jim Colosimo
SHOE-SHINE: Did you know Diamond Jim, sir?
AL: Know him? I shot him!
SHOE-SHINE: (dives back to his work a little impressed) Jeez!
AL: Remember kid there are two kinds of people in this world. The Doers and the Wa. . . No the Winners and the Losers. What are you kid?
SHOE-SHINE: I guess I'm a loser, sir.
AL: No Gino! You are a winner. No one's tryin' to cheat or kill ya. You sleep at nights. Me. Sometimes I don' even know who I am
    (There is a load cymbal crash)
AL: Hey what is that?
SHOE-SHINE: It's Wall Street crashing, Mr Capone
AL: Yea? I didn't like that noise. It sounded like the bottom fallin' outa da booze business. Here kid (gives him a 'C' note). Git!
SHOE-SHINE: Thank you sir. Mr Capone (sees the value of 100 dollar bill) Jeez!
    (As the boy exits we hear stage right a voice upstage from the shadows)
VOICE FROM THE SHADOW: Stand still and do not move (AL freezes) You have exactly six thirsty thirty-eights pointing at your black heart, Scarface Capone!
AL: (putting hand to his scar as G-MAN points a piece of timber to which are attached six thirty-eights in a row). What is this? Who are you palookas?
    (The following scene is 'cod')
VOICE IN THE SHADOW: Federal agents, scum. Created to enforce law and order and to bring purity and respect once again to the city of Chicago. My name is Eliot (Batman music) Ness!
AL: G-Men!
NESS: Exactly, gruesomegangster and now we are taking you in
AL: O yeah(he runs at the G-MAN with fist raised)
NESS: Do not lay one foolish finger on this federal force fool
AL: Huh?
NESS: We are the (batman music) "Untouchables"
AL: You can't lay any rap on me, Ness. I'm innocent. I never hoit anybody in my life. I love my wife and kid too much to do that sort of thing
NESS: Peace! Cringing criminal. We have washed out your wino warehouses, checked your faked fink finances and find you wanting!
AL: I ain't got no money. I gave it all to the poor. Look

NEWSPANEL ... 1930 CAPONE OPENS FREE SOUP KITCHENS FOR UNEMPLOYED ...

I am a public (batman music) benefactor
NESS: Trite trivia and tax evasive evidence Capone. You have no money? Then we charge you with being a vagrant! One without visible means of support!
Put the binding bracelets on his bones (The G-MAN does this)
AL: (to audience) You know there's a lotta grief attached to bein' in da limelight

EXHIBIT EIGHTEEN: 'THE COURTROOM'

As AL turns, the lights come up on a busy courtroom, people arriving and settling. AL is surrounded by SOB SISTERS who fire questions at him. Some take photographs. There is busy Court music)

SOB-SISTER 1: Mr Capone what will you wear in court?
AL: Nuddin!
SOB-SISTER 2: Our readers would love to know if it's true you're gonna divorce Mae Coughlin?
AL: No comment
SOB-SISTER 3: Has the life of your son been threatened?
AL: Who said that?
SOB-SISTER 4: Is it true that Warner Brothers wish to sign you up as star in their new movie 'Public Enemy'?
AL: I've always been a star!
SOB-SISTER 4: (writing down) He's always been a star ...
(The SOB-SISTERS rush into court)
AL: (to audience) Jeez, you'd think Mussolini was passin' through!
(AL goes to table set stage right centre already at the table are GUSIK and CAPONE's defence counsel MICHAEL AHERNE. Centre stage raised is FEDERAL COURT JUDGE WILKERSON and left DISTRICT ATTORNEY GEORGE JOHNSON. A jury line the wing up and downstage — stage right and there is a witness box area on the lower raised area stage left)
JOHNSON: The court will rise for Federal Court Judge Wilkerson on this the Fourteenth of October 1931. This court is now in session
WILKERSON: (reading sheet) Before we proceed with this case — it has come to my notice over the past few weeks that the defendant Capone has attempted to make some kind of bargain with the Mayor of Chicago, Big Bill Thompson. I am delighted to inform you that that particular political snake has been scorched

> NEWSPANEL ... 1931 THOMPSON DEFEATED ...

The jury 'fixed' by Mr Capone for some 50,000 dollars has been completely changed and a new untainted jury sworn in. This case will now proceed in a proper manner
AL: Your honour may I speak
WILKERSON: You may — if it has some bearing upon this case
AL: Your honour. You're a busy man. I'm a busy man. (laughter) There are a lot of overheads in my profession. I cannot afford to lose all this time in court cases. There is work to be done. So bearing this in mind. I would like to make the Federal Government the following very generous

> NEWSPANEL ... CAPONE OFFERS FEDERAL GOVT $1,500,00 BRIBE TO SETTLE OUT OF COURT

offer O.K. The money to be delivered in bona fide cash.
WILKERSON: Mr Capone! Your offer is unequivocally refused! And do not at any other time attempt to belittle the honesty of this courtroom. You will be seated
AL: What's the matter wid dis guy?
WILKERSON: I call Mr Johnson, Federal District Attorney to present his public prosecution

JOHNSON: Thank you your honour. I should like to present in evidence these Chicago Citizens, each will verify that sums of money were paid by the defendant. Vast sums of money not accounted for in his tax returns

CITIZEN: (Appears in the witness box. This actor plays all the roles, he/she dives down in the witness box and re-appears with different hats and voices. It should be quick and funny. Rim shots signal the appearance of each character)

TAILOR: (French) He bought two hundred suits for a thousand dollars

SHIRTS: (Jewish) Twenty five dollars he is paying for shirts, monogrammed already

JEWELLER: (German) Zirty diamunt belt buckles at two hundred unt twenty dollar a time Jah!

AUTOMOBILES: (Irish) Bejeesus he laid out twenty thousand darlin' greenbacks on my automobiles. It's the way I sell 'em

BOXING: (American) (nose pressed in) Ten fousand dollars for boxing tickets

UNDERWEAR: (Chinese) Mistee Caponi buy flom us — flifty suits of silk underwear, all made of flinest silk — like used for making pletty ladies gloves

    (The court laugh at Capone's affectation)

AL: Get him outa here (angry)

WILKERSON: Silence. I think we have heard enough thank you Mr Johnson to formulate a fairly clear picture of Mr Capone's spending and private affairs. Now Mr Aherne, I believe that on this final day you wish, in desperation, to call three character witnesses?

AHERNE: That is correct your honour. Unfortunately two of them are unable to appear

WILKERSON: They are?

AHERNE: Mr Scalise and Mr Anselmi

WILKERSON: Their profession?

AHERNE: Medical men your honour

WILKERSON: Yes, I believe this court has witnessed one or two of their recent operations. Why have they failed to appear?

AL: (leaping up) Cos' I didn't trust those two torpedoes no more!

WILKERSON: Quiet please (Friends of AL tell him not to betray himself)

AHERNE: Er they were found dead this morning, your honour

WILKERSON: What an upsetting blow for the medical profession — How did this tragic accident occur?

AHERNE: They were tapped on the head with baseball bats your honour

WILKERSON: Oh I see. Stroked to death

AHERNE: Something like that your honour. But we would still like to call Mr Capone's closest business associate, Miss Goldie Kandinski

WILKERSON: I see. And which profession does Miss Kandinski adhere to. A brain specialist?

AHERNE: No, your honour. Miss Kandinski is Mr Capone's personal elocution teacher

WILKERSON: Oh really. Is that what they call it now?

AHERNE: Call Miss Goldie Kandinski

    (GOLDIE enters the witness box)

WILKERSON: Miss Kandinski, will you please identify yourself

GOLDIE: (takes powder compact from bag looks in mirror) Yup. That's me O.K.

AHERNE: Miss Kandinski. Is it true that you have been -- intimately — related to the accused Mr Capone for the last eight years?

GOLDIE: Huh?

WILKERSON: Miss Kandinski, did you sleep with this man, Capone?

GOLDIE: (lecherously) No your honour — not a wink

    (COURTROOM laughs)

WILKERSON: (banging table) Silence in court. I have had enough of this stupidity. This case has become a travesty

GOLDIE: Did I do somethin' wrong?

WILKERSON: Sit down, madame and shut up!

GOLDIE: You too, huh?

WILKERSON: (picking up summation) Alphonse Capone of the Four Deuces Wabash Avenue and the Hawthorne Hotel, Cicero, after months of analysis of the bank books held by your so-called financial adviser, Mr. Gusik — we have discovered that they are full of disguised entries and false figures. You have over a decade, through the trade of illegal distilling, gambling, speakeasies, casinos, protection rackets and prostitution, amassed some $120,000,000 dollars that you cannot account for

AL: I'm a spendthrift (to the court who laugh)

WILKERSON: Silence! Capone have you anything sensible to say before this court passes sentence on your undoubted guilt?

AL: Yea. Sure I got somethin' to say. You newspaper people get all a dis down (the SOB SISTERS will scribble throughout) Jack, gimme dat impromptu speech you wrote me. (He reads haltingly) "All these charges is ridiculous — I am a good husband and I have a wife and kids I idolise. If I could go to Florida with them and forget it all, I would be the happiest man in the world. I want peace and I am willing to live and let live." (Throws away speech)
Time was when I had every one of you cops and judges in my pocket — yea and I supplied you with booze for your fancy parties. (The speech becomes feeling)
It's utterly impossible for a man of my age to have done all the things with which I am charged (he has put down the paper now and is talking from the heart) I'm a spook! Born of a million minds. Yet if I am found guilty, who is gonna suffer eh? The ghost or the man? You're right — it'll be me that goes to the state pen. Time was I could go anywhere and say 'hi — everyone' (he looks at the court) and you'd all shout back ... (There is total silence in the room) Yea well ... What a life! (AL slumps down into his seat again — he is a broken man)

WILKERSON: (There is a moment), (Clearing his throat) Capone will you please stand. Alphonse Capone you have been found guilty on the charge of tax evasion from 1925 to 27 and for failing to file returns for the years 28 and 29. We are tired of your consistent and flagrant abuse of our laws and therefore it is the duty of this court to see that you are punished — severely. Here is your sentence

> NEWSPANEL ... FINED $500,000 ... COSTS $30,000 ... SENTENCE — 11 YEARS! ...

(There is a gasp round the courtroom. AL sits down shaken, very slowly)

WILKERSON: This court is now dismissed and this case closed. (He hits the table three times)
(The COMPANY go out slowly and strike set as they go. AL walks towards MAE but a cop prevents him and leads him out. MAE, GUSIK, AHERNE and GOLDIE come downstage)

MAE: Thank you Mr Aherne for all your help. I know you tried to do your best

AHERNE: I am only sorry I could not have done more, Mrs Capone, but in the end we were only clutching at straws

GOLDIE: Yea dat's allright already ... Sorry

MAE: Mr Gusik, will you please see that Mr Aherne is paid his full fee — in cash
(GUSIK opens one side of his jacket to reveal many inside pockets loaded with dollars)

AHERNE: I would prefer the payment in Swiss Francs, Mrs Capone. You understand?

MAE: Of course. Jack. Foreign currency please (GUSIK opens opposite side of jacket to reveal foreign currency. He hands wad to AHERNE)

GUSIK: I think you will find the full amount plus expenses. Goodbye Mr Aherne and thank you

AHERNE: Mrs Capone (He tips hat), Mr Gusik. (To GOLDIE) Miss ..er. .thingy. (He exits)

GOLDIE: I think he likes me

GUSIK: Shall I prepare for the appeal?

MAE: (tired) Whatever you think best, Jack — eleven years is a long time to wait for a special kinda guy

GUSIK: I am deeply sorry (He goes)

GOLDIE: You know Mae, I'm choked up about everything and ... everything, you know

MAE: It's O.K. Goldie — You and I weren't the only woman in his life. It's best not to ask questions or expect too much. Oh he gave me a letter to give you

GOLDIE: Really. For me? (She opens it and reads with difficulty)
"Goldie kid, 'That's nice'. We ain't ever gonna meet again that's for sure — but let me give you somethin' before you go. You meant a lot to me, Goldie, and Mae has some money for you. I want you to take it, get outta Chicago and grab as much of life as you can.
P.S. Shuddup! "
Jesus. That's the saddest letter I ever had

MAE: Here Goldie. The money. Oh and he asked me to give you his lighter as a kinda keepsake (MAE clicks on the lighter)

GOLDIE: (She takes it) Thanks Mae — you're really sweet ya know. Say — look I'd like you to keep it then it would kinda make us friends. Would it?

MAE: Sure

GOLDIE: Hey I got an idea!

MAE: (To audience) She's got an idea?

GOLDIE: (To newspanel) Ticker-Tape, Ticker-Tape on da wall. Has Big Al any chance at all?

> NEWSPANEL ...NO...

GOLDIE: It wasn't a very good idea. I guess — this is really goodbye

MAE: This is really goodbye. Start runnin' Goldie and take care

GOLDIE: I will (she kisses Mae on the cheek and then runs) Hey (stopping) You know I bet that eleven years just flies by like . . .

MAE: Eleven years?

GOLDIE: Yea . . . well . . . I'll see ya O.K.? (brightly)

MAE: O.K. (GOLDIE has gone) Goodbye Goldie . . . Goodnight Al
(As MAE sings short reprise the prisoners assemble on to rostra area behind her, they stand behind grilles, which they carry in, there is a tightening spot on MAE)

REPRISE (quietly)

AND THE LITTLE ME, THAT'S ME
SAYS, NEVER 'TIL NOW
NO, NEVER 'TIL NOW
HAVE I LOVED ONE
LOVED JUST ONE
WHO MAKES ME HAPPY (She breaks up and exits)

EXHIBIT NINETEEN: 'ALCATRAZ'

As the lights fade on MAE and she exits the newspanel comes on

> NEWSPANEL ... 1934 CAPONE SENT TO ALCATRAZ ...

(Lights come up on the prisoners exercising, running drills, press-ups. The cell bars stand free on small hinged triangular support)

WARDEN JOHNSTON: Block C details halt. Stand still you worms. Stand up straight. Perooski! See to that shoe. O'Hara you are a mess (They answer yessir! to all commands) On the word 'move' you get into your cells, shakedown and sound off. Move! (The prisoners run to cells, they all beat rhythmically on cell bars with knives, cups or plates as they sound off)

JOHNSTON: Sound off!
(PRISONERS sound off by calling their number e.g. Vernon 98827!)

JOHNSTON: (when they have finished) O.K. You got a big surprise tonight kiddie winkies. Alcatraz Block C welcomes back from the Black hole the great Al Baloney.

(Capone shuffles in, he is older, broken, in dishevelled boiler suit) O.K. Move it Capone, otherwise we'll fix you a return ticket for the sweat pit. Maybe you like it down a there eh? (AL does not answer). Sit on the stool, creep!

AL: (under his breath) I'll kill ya, you bum

JOHNSTON: I'll kill ya you bum. Kill me? What with, eh? Big guns? Bang bang you're dead. Hi Everybody (falsetto)

PRISONERS: (in falsetto voices) Hi Al (They all bang their cups etc.)

AL: (like a tired old bull) Lay off will ya. I ain't feelin' so good

RAPP: He ain't feelin' so good (They all make kissing noises with their mouths)

LINDLEY: Didn't they give you chicken and champagne today Big Al?

VERNON: What's it feel like to be a nuthin' — clown?

PEROOSKI: (imitating a broad) Oh Al Will you take me down the Pink Pineapple speakeasy and we'll have some hot piano jazz and lotsa fun

AL: (putting his hands to his ears) SHUT UP!

O'HARA: Hey you betta not shoot your mouth off at us boy. (They laugh)

O'LEARY: Some of the inmates is gonna pay you a little visit in the night

RAPP: Spooks! Whooooooo!

JOHNSTON: Right. Shut it. Lights are goin' out (AL moves towards a cell). You! You stay there on the stool in the cold and start to cool off. Rapp. Vernon. Lucas. You keep a special eye on our pet gorilla tonight. O.K.?

RAPP: Coitanly Warder Johnston

VERNON: Any zink you say Warder Johnston

JOHNSTON: Wise guys

LINDLEY: Hey put a sock in it will ya. Some of us wanna sleep

O'LEARY: Yea. Pipe down

AL: (the lights dim as the men settle) Hey don' toin the lights down so low will ya

RAPP: Someone's comin' to get ya

(There are low whistles and inane giggles in the dark. These men are psychopathic)

SONG: 'ALCATRAZ BLUES'

AL: WHEN THE MAN TURNS DOWN THE LIGHT
AND I'M SITTIN' IN THE DARK
THEN THE SHADOWS ON THE WALL BECOME
THE GOOD TIMES OF MY LIFE
AND EVERY SHAPE, IS EVERY PLACE
I'VE EVER BEEN OR KNOWN
CITY LIGHTS IN DRIZZLE
AND THE STREETS I WALKED ALONE.

NOW THERE'S NO MORE HOT PIANO
PLAY-ING
JUST FOR ME
NO MORE WINE AND ROSES
NO GLITTER ON THE TREE
I'M A ONE TIME WINNER
AND A TWO-TIME LOSER
I FLEW TO NEAR THE SUN
'LIVE' IS 'EVIL' BACK TO FRONT
FOR A KING WHO'S NOW A BUM
SO CLOSE THE LID DOWN SOFTLY, BOYS
LET THE BLUES JUST FADE AWAY
COS THERE'S NEVER EVER GONNA BE
HOT PIANO
PLAYED FOR ME

> WHEN THE MAN TURNS UP THE LIGHT
> AND THE DAY IS COLD AND BRIGHT
> AND THE SHADOWS ON THE WALL BECOME
> THE PRISON OF MY LIFE
> AND EVERY BAR, IS EVERY SCAR
> I EVER CAUSED OR CUT
> WHITE FACES COLD WITH FEAR
> THAT I PAINTED RED WITH BLOOD

>> The chorus is reprised twice by PRISONERS and AL. They repeat in part harmony.
>> (At the end of the song there is a long moment we hear men sleeping then . . .)

RAPP: Al? (calling softly)
VERNON: Al Caponiiiii
LUCAS: (whistles softly)
>> (All round the block we hear little aggressive noises, metallic scraping, scratching etc.
>> Dreamlike light is green)
RAPP: (mimicking) Yea O.K. Mr Torrio sir
VERNON: Sweet dreams O'Banion
AL: Who is dat d'ere?
LUCAS: It's me
AL: Hello me. How are ya. (He thinks its MAE)
LUCAS: I'm fine. How are YOU!
>> (A strobe comes up on AL he is 'worked over' as SPOT comes up on MAE writing letter, stage right)
MAE: (fast — matter of fact) Dear Al, Baby
>> I'm glad they continue to treat you right, especially as you have been feelin' so bad lately. The one thing I hate when I visit is the fact that I can see you and you're so close, but I can't touch you. Never mind — it's such a short time — Aherne says that the early release is going through. Come home then, Al. Do some of that farming and fishing you promised yourself. Sonny sends his love. He's a real bright boy, doing well at school, and he asks after his big Poppa every day. He says he wants to go to Yale and become a lawyer. I think he'd be a good one, don't you? Next time I see you — it will be to take you home . . . God bless and all my love. Mae (SPOT fades)
>> (AL is doubled up on the floor, he is unconscious, a doctor comes in and kneels beside him accompaneid by Warder Johnston)
DR TWITCHELL: Warder Johnston this man is very ill — this is the fifth beating he has taken in the past three months. Are you doing your duty with any kind of vigilance?
JOHNSTON: Oh sure, Doc. I give 'him' very special attention (Prisoners laugh and hit bars)
DR TWITCHELL: You men, keep quiet!
JOHNSTON: O.K. Knock it off. Playtime's over
DR TWITCHELL: I've given him a thorough examination and he will be fit to leave today. Just. Capone is anyone coming for you?
AL: Yea (He holds ribs and jaw. He is hurt bad)
JOHNSTON: His wife is collecting him
DR TWITCHELL: Well Capone you have no bones broken but I am afraid there is something medically more serious
AL: Whatja talkin' about?
DR TWITCHELL: I'm afraid that there is an advance state in the damage
AL: Damage from what?
LINDLEY: Capone here's your gear. Your wife's arrived. Some looker (all the inmates wolf whistle). The Governor has given you clearance. You can leave whenever you like, you lucky sonofabitch.

AL: (stands very still as they all do). At last I'm finished wid all dis. I'm forty years of age but I've lived a thousand. Doc tell the paper men not to print a line about my release. I wanna go quiet. Dat's da way I feel. No more brass bands for me O.K.?
DR TWITCHELL: If that is your wish
AL: O.K. Johnston. Get me outa here. (He grabs his kit bag and exits)
JOHNSTON: Take him away, Lindley

> NEWSPANEL ... 1939 CAPONE RELEASED AFTER 8 YEARS ...

JOHNSTON: Doc what was all that serious damage stuff you was givin' Capone?
DR TWITCHELL: I'm afraid that the seeds of his sin have finally flowered. Deadly Nightshade. Capone is suffering the effects of too many good times and good time girls
JOHNSTON: Er... I don't grab ya Doc
DR TWITCHELL: Red Light Measles my friend. Syphilis. It is certain that in a fairly short time his brain will grind to a halt. Al Bananas
JOHNSTONE: You mean he'll end up a bigger screwball than when he was runnin' Chicago?
DR TWITCHELL: If he's lucky he may be able to see and hear for a few more years — after that he'll be like a wasp in a jam-jar
JOHNSTON: I never liked the creep — but I got the rotten sensation that what I feel at the moment is called compassion
DR TWITCHELL: (Picking up bag and going) He will need much of that my friend... He will need much of that (Prisoners start to quietly rattle mugs)
JOHNSTON: Shut up will ya! (Lights fade and prisoners exit with cages). Move it outa here! All prisoners into the exercise yard. Move!
PRISONER: Terrific there's gonna be a party

EXHIBIT TWENTY: 'THE BIG SLEEP'

As the lights fade on the prisoners, they rise to reveal Miami garden furniture. U.S.R. MAE wheels AL in on MOMMA CAPONE'S wheelchair. Birds sing. It's a nice day. AL wears dark glasses. He is ill. There is a blanket over his legs. On the table is a box of cigars and a lighter. One magazine

MAE: (stops the chair) It's a lovely day (long pause)
AL: (slowly) Sure
MAE: (moving downstage) You see. Momma's chair did come in useful after all
AL: Yea. That crazy woman is runnin' round the pool wid Rudy and I'm stuck here — looking at you. (He takes her hand — there is a moment) You're beautiful, kid. I'm a lucky gangster
MAE: Flattery will get you (kisses the top of his head) everywhere. Would you like a drink? A read of the paper?
AL: Huh? No. No. I'm happy just sittin'
MAE: (watches him awhile) Head O.K.?
AL: Notta good. That's how you get rewarded for bein' a hard workin' crook. I did too much thinkin' while I was at the top
MAE: You let too many people use you Al. You took the blame for a whole lotta things you never did
AL: Dat's a right. The cops and Feds hung everythin' on me but the Chicago Fire. (pause) I feel cold
MAE: I'll get you another blanket (As she goes he stops her and holds her arm — he seems to want to say something affectionate)
AL: Sure (He releases her and she walks — then turns)
MAE: You gotta take care (She exits)
AL: (He wheels himself down to the very edge of the stage) I'm glad to have this last chance to talk to you. Cos pretty soon, as you can guess, the Big Man in da sky is gonna turn out da light. And I wanted to take dis opportunity to answer the question that all you good American citizens is asking. How could you have allowed me to build my wicked empire? Dat's a easy. Cos too many

of you wanted what I had to offer. Sure you didn't like the way I went about it. But when you saw da merchandise. The booze, the casinos, the whores . . . you all came runnin'. Dat is why, when I am gone, another will take my place. That is why when you are all forgotten, I will be remembered.

Fifty years from now you ask any kid from Hong Kong to Honolulu — 'Who was Al Capone?' and he'll go 'Rat-tat-tat-tat . . .
  (REPRISE OFFSTAGE last verse of 'GONNA BEND A NEW SHAPE')

AL: (over words of song). Yea. I put a nickel in the fate machine. I watched the pin ball rollin' and I lit that million dollar star. As a matter of fact it was two hundred million (he chuckles) Mae is dat you? (He senses a presence)
MAE: It's me. I brought you another blanket
AL: Baby?
MAE: Yea?
AL: My head hurts muchly. I think that I will sleep now. You know?
MAE: Yea. Sure. I know
AL: Maybe one last cigar
MAE: (She hands him one from the box and lights it) Here
AL: (holds her wrist as he recognises GOLDIE'S lighter) Hey that's . . .
MAE: She wanted me to have it
AL: She was a gooda kid
  (CHORUS SING OFFSTAGE 'If you close your eyes you can really see it
              When you fall asleep you can really dream it.')
MAE: (Mimics GOLDIE) Yea. Dat's right already
AL: I feel very tired (slowly)

> NEWSPANEL . . . A KIND KINDA GUY . . . THE KINDA GUY THAT KILLS . . .

MAE: You sleep Big Al
AL: Hey
MAE: Yea?
AL: Let's hope this cigar don' explode! (He chuckles then slumps)

  LIGHTS FADE OUT

  REPRISE AS CURTAIN CALL NUMBER 'CHICAGO' (All COMPANY in white fedoras and suits)

  PLAY COMPANY OFFSTAGE WITH 'RIDIN' ALONG ON LOVE'
  THE STAGE IS EMPTY

> NEWSPANEL . . . 'THE END' . . .

HOUSE LIGHTS UP

www.ingramcontent.com/pod-product-compliance
Ingram Content Group UK Ltd.
Pitfield, Milton Keynes, MK11 3LW, UK
UKHW021848210426
5322IPUK00022B/531